# Rethinking
# Patient Safety

# Rethinking Patient Safety

By Suzette Woodward

CRC Press
Taylor & Francis Group
Boca Raton London New York

CRC Press is an imprint of the
Taylor & Francis Group, an **informa** business

A PRODUCTIVITY PRESS BOOK

CRC Press
Taylor & Francis Group
6000 Broken Sound Parkway NW, Suite 300
Boca Raton, FL 33487-2742

International Standard Book Number-13: 978-1-4987-7854-1 (Hardback)

International Standard Book Number-13: 978-1-4987-7855-8 (eBook)

### Library of Congress Cataloging-in-Publication Data

Names: Woodward, Suzette, author.
Title: Rethinking patient safety / Suzette Woodward.
Description: Boca Raton : Taylor & Francis, 2017. | Includes bibliographical references.
Identifiers: LCCN 2016044132| ISBN 9781498778541 (hardback) | ISBN 9781498778558 (ebook)
Subjects: LCSH: Medical errors--Prevention. | Medical care--Quality control. | Patients--Safety measures.
Classification: LCC R729.8 .W66 2017 | DDC 610.28/9--dc23
LC record available at https://lccn.loc.gov/2016044132

**Visit the Taylor & Francis Web site at**
**http://www.taylorandfrancis.com**

**and the CRC Press Web site at**

**http://www.crcpress.com**

When you talk, you are only repeating what you already know. But if you listen, you may learn something new.

**Dalai Lama**

# Contents

# Preface

Everything we do should be about keeping patients as safe as we can, and the vast majority of healthcare is provided safely and effectively. However, just like any high-risk industry, things can and do go wrong.

I have worked for the last two decades of my career in the field of patient safety, and despite efforts across the globe, progress towards safer healthcare has been slow and in many areas lasting change has yet to be realised. Don Berwick (2015) says that if you are climbing a mountain and you find an impasse, don't sit there waiting for the situation to change. If you stay, it will almost definitely lead to your demise. However, you also can't try to break your way through – it will likely be impossible to do that. The answer is to forget that people may look down on you for failing, forget that it may damage your self-esteem and reputation. There is no shame in saying you are defeated. What we all need to do in that situation is to find another way. Climb down, look back at what we now know, look at all the evidence around us and plot the next path. By doing that, we have already learnt one valuable lesson about the route we will not be taking. So in order for us to achieve patient safety, I think we need to look at all our previous efforts that meant we didn't quite get there; we reached an impasse. Look at all the evidence we have around us, and plot a new path.

Stopping or doing things in a very different way always sounds like such a big deal. It sounds like something that should be approached with awe and done once or twice in a lifetime. We fear it will make us look stupid. I would argue that rethinking patient safety is a very wise thing to do. I am someone who needs more out of a career than a job. I need to feel as if everything I do is in sync with my strong value systems. Accordingly, I have chosen a career that has become my life – to support a quest to do something meaningful, that of improving the safety of patient care. I will not be content until we have plotted the next path, rapidly started to climb and, if possible, ascended further than we ever have before.

*Rethinking Patient Safety* is a culmination of the learning to date. It provides insight from myself and others on why we have not achieved the anticipated or desired outcomes. It then makes the case for how we need to rethink and redesign fundamental aspects of the current approach to patient safety, but also provides the reader with a potential way forward – the profoundly simple method of facilitated safety conversations.

This book is for all the patient safety mountain climbers who are willing to take that journey towards something meaningful. People who are new to the subject and those who have made a few ascents already: all I hope is that it helps you with a few steps towards the top and that you enjoy it along the way.

**Suzette Woodward**

# Acknowledgements

This book is thanks to all those who taught me so much; those who dedicate their careers to improving the safety of patient care. Thanks in particular to those who don't want to wait a moment and are eager to change the world around them: Shelly Jeffcott, Carl Macrae, Charles Vincent, Rene Amalberti, Don Berwick and Eric Hollnagel, to name a few. Particular thanks to Scott Morrish, who has moved and motivated me in equal measure.

To those I have worked with over the 35 years of my career, thank you. I have worked with the most astonishing people, none more so than the most joyous team anyone could have to work alongside – the Sign up to Safety team, a wonderful, inspiring group of people: Dane Wiig, Cat Harrison, Hannah Thompson, Adam Mohammed, Catherine Ede, Jane Reid, Owen Bennett, Anna Babic, David Naylor and Sarah Garrett. The final two chapters are very much down to their brilliance – I just get to be the scribe.

Finally, this book is dedicated to Bradley, without whom there would be no book. You have been a constant source of inspiration, ideas and knowledge and have been there for me every step of the way. You are in every beat of my heart. Thank you.

# Introduction

I believe we can change the world if we start listening to one another again.

**Margaret Wheatley**
*2009*

Healthcare has been transformed over the centuries – it is now extremely complex, and in turn has become stressful, pressured and increasingly faster-paced. Time in healthcare has come to be one of the most precious resources. Along the way, we have lost the very essence of what we were trying to do in those early transformative years.

Healthcare, as an industry, is no different from any other high-risk industry; the very people who are treated and cared for by the industry are also at risk of harm. Harm that is caused by the treatment or care provided, as opposed to harm caused by the natural course of the patient's original illness or condition. The field of patient safety has grown out of this knowledge and seeks to figure out why harm happens and what we can do to minimise it happening as well as minimising its effect.

Over the last two decades, in particular, significant efforts have been made to learn as much as we can about the system, the way in which human beings make errors and mistakes and how the system could be set up to help humans be safer. We have focused predominantly on hospital care and interventions that reduce harm, topic by topic. We have also focused on capturing significant amounts of data in the hope that these data will tell us where we should prioritise our efforts. However, this cacophony of mostly top-down interventions has led to people feeling drowned by instruction. In particular, people have got fed up with change, fed up with new interventions surpassing the others, fed up with moving on to something new before something has finished. There have been a variety of solutions: interventions, research, improvement projects, innovative products, tons of guidance, standards and national initiatives. Some were initially borrowed from other high-risk industries (such as aviation or nuclear power); others, as the science grew, were specifically developed by and for healthcare. This whole approach has tired people out, turned them off. People are also fed up of being told what to do. Change only happens when everyday people want it to, not when someone decides they have to. People are also becoming increasingly isolated and polarised from each other.

Our efforts, though, have been a touch random – we give the impression that we don't quite know where to start or what to focus on when. We have also not consolidated our actions in that we have moved from one thing to another and then another. Successes are there, but it feels like there are many more failures. As a result, patients are still being harmed unnecessarily. As you read this sentence, someone will have been given the wrong medication, been misdiagnosed, contracted an infection or fallen out of bed. The efforts over the last two decades to improve patient safety do not seem to have made many inroads and the same things are still happening now as they were over 20 years ago. We have not yet created a comprehensive, systematic approach to patient safety.

We need to rethink patient safety. If we were to make a fresh start, what would that look like? I would argue that we need to go back to the fundamentals. Ask ourselves some difficult questions, the kind of questions that you can, in fact, ask after you have tested interventions or ideas and assumptions. So while we may be disappointed in our efforts so far, perhaps it is only through these experiences that we can finally see what we might want to do or where we now should be focusing. Experiential learning is the very best form of learning. Therefore, this is a brilliant time to rethink patient safety, learning from and building on our collective experiences across the field of patient safety over the last two decades.

Experiential learning focuses on the learning process for the individual through observation and interaction as opposed to reading from a book. Thus, one makes discoveries and experiments with first-hand knowledge instead of hearing or reading about others' experiences. Kolb (1984) talks about moving from concrete experience to reflective observation and then abstract conceptualisation, which leads to active experimentation. This book explores our concrete experiences over the last two decades and provides my own personal reflective observations as well as those of others who have also worked in the field of patient safety during this time. Reflection is a crucial part of the experiential learning process. The book also explores a particular concept to consider for the future and shares the story of Sign up to Safety, which is experimenting with this concept to provide people with concrete experiences.

The final part of the book sets out the case for the profoundly simple concept of wanting people to talk to each other about what they know about keeping patients safer. To paraphrase Margaret Wheatley, I believe that we can change the world of safety if we start listening to one another again. Listening to another human being starts to create a relationship, starts to help us understand them more. Listening means we hear someone else's point of view rather than forcing our own onto others. We move away from our judgments and assumptions towards curiosity. This means we start to learn more about what could be safer, what could or should be changed. The reason why I believe this so fervently is that 'not listening', 'not being heard' or 'not being able to speak out' has led to harm on so many occasions. Throughout this book, you will notice the role that conversations have played in both hindering and helping the safety of patient care.

Each chapter has a suggested reading list of the books that will provide readers with further detail associated with the chapter's theme. There are additional references throughout that are found at the end of the book in the usual way.

The following is an outline of the chapters ahead:

Chapter 1 sets the scene, explains what patient safety is and provides an overview of the growth of patient safety from the early pioneers of the 1850s to today, in 2016.

Chapter 2 describes the scale of the problem and the challenges of measuring avoidable harm.

Chapter 3 explores the culture of learning using three contrasting stories of the response to learning from harm.

Chapter 4 outlines the system approach to safety and provides the reader with brief insights into the concepts of resilience, lessons from other high-risk industries, human factors, a proactive approach to safety called 'Safety II' and the latest thinking from experts such as Hollnagel, Vincent and Amalberti.

Chapter 5 summarises what an ideal safety culture should look like, based on the just culture principles, and explores the three aspects of human behaviour at the heart of patient safety: human error, risky behaviour and reckless behaviour.

Chapter 6 discusses the problem with traditional methods in patient safety with a particular focus on incident reporting.

Chapter 7 focuses on risk management and incident investigation and makes the case for bringing to the forefront the forgotten discipline of risk management and the importance of having skilled individuals to conduct incident investigations.

Chapter 8 shares stories that illustrate the heartbreaking impact on front-line workers.

Chapter 9 explains the importance of implementation and how as much effort should be given to implementation as it is to innovation. The chapter provides examples that illustrate that it is never as simple as just telling people to 'get on with it'.

Chapter 10 provides the reader with a variety of things they can do differently to improve the implementation of safer practices.

Chapter 11 brings together the latest thinking on what could be done differently over the next 15 years and beyond.

Chapter 12 describes the story of Sign up to Safety, a patient safety campaign set up to build a bottom-up approach to patient safety leadership, ownership and improvement.

Chapter 13 shares our moment of illumination, how we have moved from reflective observation to abstract conceptualisation of a particular approach – and our campaign throughline – which could be described as 'profoundly simple', that of wanting people to talk to each other about what they know about making care safer.

Chapter 14 provides the case that simple conversations between one human being and another are at the heart of patient safety; that conversations will help us notice, understand and learn about how we can achieve the safest and best possible care for patients.

Chapter 15 describes the work that the Sign up to Safety campaign team has been doing to explore a method for a structured and facilitated conversation as a way of bringing people together to discover how we can make care safer.

# Author

**Suzette Woodward** is a paediatric intensive care nurse who has worked for 35 years in the National Health System (NHS) in the UK, for the last two decades at a national level in patient safety. Suzette has worked as a board director at the National Patient Safety Agency and the NHS Litigation Authority, both in the UK.

She has led the national Sign up to Safety campaign since 2014, working across the NHS in England to focus on the creation of a just safety culture. While working full time, Suzette achieved a distinction for her master's degree in clinical risk and a doctorate in patient safety that won the university prize of the year. Over the last few years, Suzette has been named by her peers as one of the most inspirational women in the NHS in 2013, top nursing leader in 2014 and top clinical leader in 2015.

# Chapter 1

# Patient Safety

Medicine used to be simple, ineffective and relatively safe. It is now complex, effective and potentially dangerous.

**Sir Cyril Chantler**
*1999*

## What Is Patient Safety?

The science of patient safety is relatively young. Early pioneers identified aspects of safety in the 1850s, but the science as we know it today grew substantially from around the mid-1990s. Patient safety is not a task or a set of technical interventions – it is a mindset, it is in everything we do. Feeling safe is one of the most important needs for our patients. Feeling safe and being safe. The act of keeping patients safe is about being constantly vigilant; noticing what happens every moment of every day, noticing when it goes right, noticing when it could go wrong and noticing when it does go wrong. With that knowledge, we then constantly adapt our behaviour and practice; constantly refine our performance or our way of working so that it gets safer and safer and safer. Patient safety is about making small incremental improvements in any process that add up to a significant improvement when they are all added together. It is not about a single solution, a single person or a one-size-fits-all approach.

In my view, there is a fundamental difference between patient safety and quality. Patient safety is not a subset of quality – it is a unique science, a specialist field of healthcare that applies safety science methods towards the goal of achieving a safer system. Safety is not the same as quality, nor is it the same as effectiveness or reliability. Healthcare can be of high quality but unsafe; it can be effective and reliable but unsafe. It can also be safe but of poor quality, ineffective or unreliable. There are unique aspects to patient safety that are not generally thought of as about quality improvement. These includes aspects such as preventative risk analysis and designing equipment and systems to make them easy and intuitive to use and as error-proof as possible, as well as using investigative methodologies to truly understand why things go wrong.

The focus seems to have shifted away from understanding human error and risk, two vital components of patient safety, to a focus on quality and quality improvement. This is diverting attention from the unique and specific aspects of patient safety that require addressing; it is also diverting policy, research and resources away from safety and safety improvement. The quest for safety is not in opposition to pursuing other aspects of quality, effectiveness or experience, for example, but there is a need for a distinct and separate focus on safety rather than it being simply a component of quality. Safety is an essential building block for achieving high performance in all other areas. We dilute its importance by focusing on quality instead.

Despite all the hard or technical barriers we can put in place, we are human and we are frequently reminded of our human fallibility when we make mistakes or errors, slips or lapses. At the very heart of safety is keeping people safer; people are usually the final barrier between a safe act and an unsafe act. In most industries, and in particular healthcare, people are dependent on other people. How those people get on, interact, communicate and work together can make or break safety. The problem is we have not focused enough on helping these people be safer and creating relationships that enhance safety; we have focused too much on the technical and not enough on the non-technical aspects of patient safety.

What does safe look like? First, we will never be safe. As Professor James Reason says in the foreword to *Close Calls* (Macrae 2014b), there are not enough trees in the rainforest to write a set of procedures that will guarantee freedom from harm. Healthcare will always carry risks; human beings are fallible. However, harm to patients should not be viewed as an acceptable part of modern healthcare. Unsafe care results in far too many individual tragedies every year, with both patients and those who provide their care suffering as a consequence. If we are to save more lives and significantly reduce avoidable patient harm, there is a need for a change in perspective. It's needed because it is also personal. We and our families and friends could be the next ones affected. It's needed because knowingly offering a patient unsafe care is morally and ethically wrong. Healthcare is a safety-critical industry and patient safety must be our core business.

## Pioneers

There are undoubtedly many unsung and unpublished individuals who have noticed aspects of poor patient safety and attempted to change behaviour and practice in order to minimise harm to patients. For all those who have not been recognised, there have been a few in our history who have been noticed and these include the early pioneers of patient safety such as Florence Nightingale, Ignaz Semmelweis, Ernst Codman and Herbert William Heinrich.

Nightingale is clearly known for being at the forefront of nursing and nurse training, but she is also one of the earliest patient safety thinkers and statisticians. Measurement experts today would love the fact that Florence Nightingale regarded statistics as the foundation for change and the most important science in the whole world. In the mid-1850s, she noticed that many of the soldiers were dying in ways that she intuitively thought were avoidable. She plotted all of the reasons why soldiers died in the army in the Crimean War from April 1854 to March 1855 and found that most of the soldiers' illnesses were caused by what she describes as 'defects in the system'. She deduced that perhaps at least one in seven of the patients (around 14%) died from preventable diseases rather than their battle wounds. As a result of this work, she made huge improvements to the way the soldiers were being cared for. These were not isolated interventions but fundamental aspects of care: good nutrition, warm clothing and good ventilation, and most importantly, cleanliness and hand hygiene (Huxley 1975).

Ignaz Semmelweis was a Hungarian physician who, also in the 1850s, around the same time as Nightingale, wanted to understand why some of his patients died after childbirth. The detailed story of Semmelweis and his relentless pursuit of addressing maternal deaths is a fascinating one and this summary really only skims the surface of his story. Not only are the lessons from this story relevant to patient safety but they are also pertinent for anyone trying to convince others to change and trying to be heard.

Semmelweis worked in one of the first obstetric clinics in Vienna. These institutions had been set up all over Europe to provide free care, which made them attractive to 'under-privileged' women, including prostitutes. In return for the free services, the women would be subjects for the training of doctors and midwives. In his first publication, Semmelweis (1857) describes the tale of two maternity clinics at the Viennese hospital that he worked at. The first clinic had an average death rate from an infection called puerperal fever of around 10%. The second clinic's rate was lower, averaging less than 4%. Interestingly, this fact was known outside the hospital and the women begged to be admitted to the second clinic. Semmelweis described how desperate women were begging on their knees not to be admitted to the first clinic. In fact, some women even preferred to give birth in the streets. Semmelweis was puzzled and deeply troubled by the fact that puerperal fever was rare among women giving street births and that the first clinic had a much higher mortality rate. The two clinics used almost the same techniques, and Semmelweis started a meticulous process of eliminating all possible differences between them. He excluded a variety of potential causes; the only major difference was the individuals who worked there. The first clinic was the teaching service for medical students, while the second clinic had been selected in 1841 for the instruction of midwives only.

In 1847, one of his friends died after being accidently stabbed by a student's scalpel while performing a postmortem. The friend died of the same puerperal fever that the women were dying from. He proposed that the cause was, in fact, the doctors and medical students, who were routinely moving from the task of dissecting corpses to examining new mothers without first washing their hands. They transferred infections from the corpses to the mothers, causing their deaths as a consequence. The midwives were not engaged in autopsies. He issued a policy of washing hands between autopsy work and the examination of patients. The result was that the mortality rate in the first clinic dropped by 90%. When the doctors, medical students and midwives washed their hands, the number of deaths from infections went down.

What happened next is as interesting as his findings. Despite what appears to be compelling evidence and results that reduced mortality to below 1% from that of between 10% and 35%, his observations conflicted with the established views at the time. His ideas were rejected. Semmelweis not only failed to convince his colleagues enough to change their practice, he angered and offended them. In fact, there is today a phrase that has been used to describe his challenge, which is named after him: the *Semmelweis reflex*. This is used as a metaphor for human behaviour that is characterised by a reflex-like rejection of new knowledge because it contradicts entrenched norms and beliefs (Leary 1991). As he grew more frustrated and angry at what he felt was a disregard for people's lives, he grew more and more erratic and he even at one point called his colleagues murderers. Semmelweis was truly misunderstood and undervalued for his work. He only really earned widespread acceptance years after his death at the age of 47. He died of septicaemia only 14 days after being committed to a mental health institution.

Ernest Codman was a pioneering Boston surgeon who graduated from Harvard Medical School in 1895 and worked at Massachusetts General Hospital. He was interested in why patients died, and kept track of every patient outcome (Donabedian 1989, Berwick 1989). He followed up every patient for at least a year to observe long-term outcomes and to identify 'clinical misadventures'. He believed that all his information should be made public so that patients could choose which doctors and hospitals they were treated at. He also was not listened to by his colleagues and eventually had to establish his own hospital to implement his improvement methods. Not only did he publish the deaths, he also published his opinions on whether they could have been prevented. Of 337 patients discharged between 1911 and 1916, Codman recorded and published 123 errors. He tried to understand what the possible causes of these errors were and set up group conversations about these outcomes through the use of morbidity and mortality meetings. This is an early example of the use of conversations and storytelling in patient safety.

Herbert William Heinrich was born in 1886. He was an American industrial safety pioneer who created the domino model, which was published in 1931. Heinrich compared the sequence of an incident to a row of dominos, and that if one domino falls, it automatically knocks down its neighbour and so on until they all fall (and the injury or incident occurs) (Leveson 2012). Heinrich's sequence started with the environment, then the person and then the unsafe act, leading to accident and injury. Heinrich's Law is named after him: in a workplace, for every accident that causes a major injury, there are 29 accidents that cause minor injuries and 300 accidents that cause no injuries. Heinrich expressed this idea in a safety pyramid in 1959 (Heinrich 1959, Roos et al. 1980). He believed that many accidents share common causes and that addressing an accident that caused no injuries could prevent an accident that did. He suggested that 95% of all workplace accidents are caused by unsafe acts by humans, and because of that he encouraged employers to put in controls in the workplace that might prevent these unsafe acts from happening.

## Over One Hundred Years Later

Literature searches relating to patient safety reveal very little until we reach the 1980s. Anaesthesiologists were the first to truly embrace the concepts of patient safety, and during the 1980s became the leading specialty to address the safety of patient care. This work significantly reduced the risks associated with anaesthesia, which even today is one of the safer aspects of patient care as a result. Anaesthesiologists held symposiums on deaths and injuries as well as forming the US group the Anesthesia Patient Safety Foundation (APSF) in 1984. This, interestingly, may well be the first use of the term patient safety. In 1989 in Australia, the Australian Patient Safety Foundation was founded in order to capture anaesthetic events and errors.

Forerunners of this period included Jens Rasmussen, James Reason, Lucian Leape, Charles Vincent and Don Berwick. These were individuals from very different backgrounds but who came to similar conclusions.

Jens Rasmussen was a systems safety and human factors professor in Denmark (Rasmussen et al. 1987). He was followed by others, including James Reason, who had worked predominantly in high-risk industries such as the nuclear industry and aviation and had written a book all about the different types of human error. Reason (1990) described why mistakes and errors happened using the now famous 'swiss-cheese' model of error. Over the subsequent 25 years, Reason has helped rewrite critical assumptions about why things go wrong and he has constantly challenged the thinking on human error and patient safety. He is an undisputed master and has a unique way of helping us understand what can and should be done.

It was really only in the 1990s that we started to understand the nature and scale of avoidable harm. We saw the rise of clinical risk management and the use of methods normally used by aviation and mechanical engineering applied to anaesthesiology.

Reason taught us that human error is the inadvertent action of doing something wrong; something that was not how it should have been done, a slip, a lapse, a mistake. He reminded us that we all make mistakes all of the time, like picking up the wrong keys, forgetting your ID, miscalculating a medication dose, missing a turn-off from the motorway, picking up strawberry yoghurt instead of raspberry or calling our children by the wrong names. Most of these errors that we make every day have generally minimal consequences. In healthcare, however, we can make similar types of errors with the potential for dire consequences.

Lucian Leape (1994) wrote about error in medicine, Charles Vincent (1995) wrote one of the first books on clinical risk management and Don Berwick is a paediatrician who studied at Harvard Medical School in Boston. In 1983, Berwick became one of the first people to hold a role in quality measurement in addition to his clinical duties. He learnt from other high-risk industries, including aviation and manufacturing.

He co-founded the Institute for Healthcare Improvement in 1989. Berwick has spoken and published widely on the subjects of quality improvement and patient safety, many of which are referenced throughout this book. All of us in safety have trailed behind these thinkers and we owe them a great debt of gratitude.

Building on the 1980s, our knowledge started to grow in the mid-1990s. For example, in 1995 in the UK, with the focus on reducing litigation claims, a national organisation, the NHS Litigation Authority (NHSLA), issued a set of risk management standards. This was a series of standards to encourage the promotion of good practice and reduce the number and value of clinical claims. They covered a variety of key risk areas such as advice and consent, health records and induction, training and competence and incident reporting.

At the turn of the twenty-first century, the spotlight on patient safety significantly increased. Two landmark documents, *To Err Is Human: Building a Safer Health System* (Institute of Medicine 1999) in the United States and 'An Organisation with a Memory', the report of the Chief Medical Officer's Expert Group (Department of Health 2000), were defining moments in the patient safety movement and focused attention on error, adverse events and harm like never before.

*To Err Is Human* declared that safety issues caused more deaths than car crashes, breast cancer or AIDS, and that they were largely preventable. It talked about establishing a national focus in the United States, with leadership, research, tools and protocols to enhance the knowledge base about safety. The report called for a nationwide public mandatory reporting system to identify and learn from errors and oversight organisations to help raise performance standards and expectations for improvements in safety.

Around this time in the UK, the Department of Health issued their own 'call to action': An organisation with a memory, which recommended the creation of a national agency and a national database to collect safety incidents from across

England and Wales (Department of Health 2000). This led to the setting up in 2001 of the National Patient Safety Agency (NPSA) and the National Reporting and Learning System (NRLS), a patient safety database designed and rolled out in 2005 that continues to this day.

## Suggested Reading

*Clinical Risk Management*, written by Charles Vincent in 1995, with a second edition in 2001. This book provides an understanding of the principles of risk management, with insight from James Reason, Kieran Walshe, Liam Donaldson, Jan Davies and others. It offers a great foundation for anyone wanting to work in or know more about risk management.

*Complications*, written by Atul Gawande in 2002, is an example of storytelling at its best; a book that truly brings to life the science of patient safety.

*Human Factors and Ergonomics in Practice: Improving System Performance and Human Well Being in the Real World* by Steven Shorrock and Claire Williams, CRC Press, Taylor and Francis Group, 2017.

*Patient Safety*, written by Charles Vincent, first published in 2006 and then updated in 2010. This book sets out the evolution of patient safety, the hazards of healthcare, an indication of the nature and scale of error and harm, systems thinking, incident investigation and potential solutions for patient safety including design, technology and standardisation. It also describes the creation of a culture of safety and patient involvement in safety.

*Safety and Ethics in Healthcare: A Guide to Getting it Right* by Bill Runciman, Alan Merry and Merrilyn Walton, published in 2007 by Ashgate Publishing, provides a practical guide to improving patient safety for clinicians.

# Chapter 2

# The Scale of the Problem

> Rather than simply trying to count and attribute the
> number of deaths to avoidable harm, reviews of
> individual deaths should focus on identifying ways of
> improving the quality and safety of care.
>
> **Helen Hogan**
> *2014*

Measuring aspects of patient safety has been a consistent challenge across healthcare. Measurement is vital if we want to know whether something has increased, stayed the same or decreased. Patient safety is no different. However, it is incredibly hard to measure improvements in patient safety, partly because we are trying to measure an absence of something.

In order to measure the scale and nature of harm in healthcare, a number of studies have been undertaken across the world. One of the first published studies into patient harm is found in the 1970s. This was a study conducted in 1974 in California, in the United States, and published in 1977. The researchers found that, out of a total of three million hospital admissions, around 5% (140,000) of them resulted in injuries, with just under 1% (24,000) of them due to negligence (Mills 1977). A later study in 1992, the Utah and Colorado study, estimated that as many as 98,000 patients in hospital settings in the United States died each year as a result of problems related to their care.

It was not until the findings of the Harvard Medical Practice Study that people started to pay attention (Brennan et al. 1991, Leape et al. 1991). This study published research that had been undertaken in 1984. The researchers studied 30,000 randomly selected discharge records from 51 New York hospitals in the United States. They found that serious adverse events (harm related to the care provided and not to the illness or disease) occurred in 3.7% of the patients in their study. Of the 3.7% adverse events, the researchers considered that 58% were attributable to error and deemed preventable and 13.6% had resulted in death.

The Harvard Medical Practice Study was a case note review. This method has been replicated and adapted in terms of its methodology across the globe. It is a method based on clinical experts' retrospective reviews of healthcare records, assessing the quality and safety of care provided during an admission. The results of these studies have identified incidences of adverse event rates across a variety of countries, ranging from 2.9% to 16.6% of all hospital admissions with those deemed preventable ranging from 1.0% to 8.6% (Vincent et al. 2001, Davis et al. 2002, Baker et al. 2004, Briant et al. 2006, Soop et al. 2009, Zegers et al. 2009).

In the UK, a study published in 2001 estimated that 1 in 10 people suffered harm in hospitals caused by a range of errors or adverse events in the course of receiving hospital care (Vincent et al. 2001). Interestingly, this was only ever meant to be a pilot study, which would have led to a much larger study across the National Health Service (NHS) in England, but the larger study was never carried out. The Vincent study, as it is now known, led to the statistic most used in relation to patient safety in the NHS: that 10% of healthcare results in harm caused by the care the patient receives and not their illness, and that half of that is avoidable.

However, case note reviews have had their fair share of critics; they only provide a snapshot of a particular episode of care and a particular time and place, and the opinions of reviewers have been found to be subjective and varied. The judgment of reviewers is described as the 'Achilles' heel' of record review studies. This variation includes the estimates of life expectancy, the subjective element in judgments of avoidability and the quality of care. For example, preventability is usually measured on a 1 to 6 Likert scale, with preventable deaths defined as those scoring 4 and above. Reviewers find it difficult to agree on these measures. There are also particular issues relating to deaths associated with unsafe care. Often, these are the deaths of patients who were very ill with an already poor prognosis regarding their original illness or condition. Reviewers find it difficult to agree on whether the death was as a result of the unsafe care or their illness.

Hogan and others have described the unreliability of even the most carefully structured case review (Lilford et al. 2007, Hogan 2015). In addition to the ones mentioned so far, Hogan (2015) lists the limitations and risks of case note reviews:

■ The quality of the case notes themselves is also an issue in that they are often incomplete.
■ Hindsight bias influences the judgment of causation and preventability.
■ Variations in the intensity of the treatment delivered to the growing population of elderly patients have the potential to impact the number of errors.
■ The small number of deaths occurring in each hospital will inevitably result in large random error around the measure, and the relatively small proportion of deaths that appear to be preventable provides further evidence that overall hospital mortality rates are a poor indicator of quality of care.
■ While the estimated number of preventable hospital deaths may prove helpful in raising interest in patient

safety and a commitment to improvement, overestimating the size of the problem and the risk to patients may induce unjustified levels of anxiety and fear among the public.

Even so, the data from these studies have been generally accepted as the best guess of how the healthcare system causes harm, even though those who worked on them have said they are likely to understate the size of the problem. Many researchers believe that avoidable harm is far higher than the research suggests. For example, more recent studies include that of Landrigan and colleagues, who reported in 2010 that 0.6% of hospital admissions in North Carolina over a 6 year period (2001 to 2007) resulted in death, and estimated that 63% of these were due to errors (Landrigan et al. 2010).

Recently, researchers from Johns Hopkins University School of Medicine estimated that clinical error is the third highest cause of death in the United States after cancer and heart disease (Makary and Daniel 2016). These researchers assert that more than 250,000 people a year died as a result of an error by the people treating them, behind heart disease (611,000 deaths) and cancer (585,000) on the list of top causes of death, but significantly ahead of the 149,000 who die from chronic respiratory disease. The researchers said they had analysed death rates in the United States between 2000 and 2008. They then calculated that 251,454 people would have died as a result of a medical error out of 35,416,020 hospital visits in 2013. That represented 9.5% of the total number of annual deaths in the United States (Makary and Daniel 2016).

Patient safety experts, Kaveh Shojania and Mary Dixon-Woods (2016), responded to the research by Makary and Daniel and questioned the conclusion. First, they say that the estimate fails the plausibility test. There are around 2.5 million deaths in the United States each year, approximately 700,000 of which occur in hospital (Hall et al. 2013). Shojania and Dixon-Woods (2016) state

> We – and many clinicians and researchers – find it very hard to believe that one in 10 of all US deaths, or a third of inpatient deaths (the 251,454 estimated by Makary and Daniel) result from "medical error".

Second, they say that the authors of the article do not provide any sort of formal methodology. Similar to a number of studies over the years, the authors extrapolated preventable death rates from those reported in other studies. Also, in another similar trait of studies related to extrapolated mortality data, the authors use the numbers to rank against other causes of death to make the case that it comes third on that list. Shojania and Dixon-Woods (2016) rightly say that these two steps are precarious mainly because the four studies used to create the estimate all have different methodologies and varying definitions with a variety of denominators across the studies.

In relation to measuring avoidable deaths, more reliable data are considered to be those of the recent studies by Helen Hogan and colleagues (2012 and 2015). Hogan and a team of researchers conducted a retrospective case record review study in the UK in 2009 (Hogan et al. 2012). In this study of 1000 adults who died in 2009 in 10 acute hospitals, the reviewers judged 5.2% of deaths as having a 50% or greater chance of being preventable. Extrapolating from these figures, the authors suggest there would have been 11,859 adult preventable deaths in hospitals in England in 2009. In this study, Hogan and her colleagues found that the problems associated with preventable deaths occurred in all phases of hospital care and involved poor clinical monitoring (31%), diagnostic errors (30%) or inadequate drug or fluid management (21%). Most preventable deaths (60%) occurred in elderly, frail patients with multiple comorbidities who were also judged to have had less than 1 year left to live (Hogan et al. 2012).

In Hogan's (2015) second study, the research was to determine the proportion of avoidable deaths in acute hospital trusts in England and to determine the association with the hospital-wide standardised mortality ratios (HSMR) and summary hospital-level mortality indicator (SHMI). The HSMR and SHMI are a case-mix adjusted ratio of 'observed' to 'expected' hospital deaths, calculated using hospital administrative data. These measures all compare each hospital with a standard ratio derived from the mean of all the ratios in the sample, which changes from year to year. HSMR and SHMI have been used for over 20 years in the UK to infer that hospitals towards the higher end of the ratio distribution have higher levels of preventable deaths.

There are international concerns about the value of HSMRs (Scott et al. 2011, Hogan et al. 2015) and these concerns focus on the multiple factors that influence the ratio: chance, adequacy of case-mix adjustment, depth and breadth of disease coding, varied admission and discharge policies, patient exclusions and local service configurations. In summary, they lack statistical and clinical credibility because the outcomes depend on how the data are collected and analysed. Some even say that HSMRs can inaccurately label good hospitals as poor performers and fail to identify many hospitals with true quality problems (Shojania 2008).

The reviewers in the second study identified a preventable death rate of 3.6%, and no significant variation in the proportion of preventable deaths between hospitals (Hogan et al. 2015). Makary and Daniel claim that medical error accounts for more than 250,000 deaths per year and therefore stands in contrast to the Hogan et al. findings. Applying the 3.6% rate of preventability to the total number of hospital deaths in the United States each year produces an estimate of about 25,200 avoidable hospital-related deaths annually, roughly 10-fold lower than the estimate by Makary and Daniel (Shojania and Dixon-Woods 2016).

In their commentary, Shojania and Dixon-Woods (2016) are concerned about making the field of patient safety all about death:

> Just as most deaths do not involve medical error, most medical errors do not produce death – but they can still produce substantial morbidity, costs, suffering and distress.

They suggest that focusing only on avoidable death risks shifting resources away from many settings of care, including almost all non-hospital settings, where death is not the most relevant outcome.

Far less is known about the nature and scale of the problem in primary care (Panesar et al. 2015). A systematic review by Panesar and colleagues (2015) found that patient safety incidents are a relatively frequent occurrence in primary care, but that most do not appear to result in significant harm to patients. The systematic review was not able to provide a point estimate of the frequency of incidents, but record review studies suggested a median of around two to three incidents per 100 consultations/patient records reviewed. About 4% of these incidents were associated with severe harm. Of these, diagnostic and medication incidents were most likely to result in harm and most likely to result in severe harm.

There are many arguments against measuring mortality as a measure of quality or safety (Shahian et al. 2010, Girling et al. 2012, Shojania 2012). In general, researchers say there is no single reliable measure to capture all preventable deaths in healthcare; for example, measuring an absence of mortality (lives saved) is virtually impossible.

Researchers also remain unconvinced of any sweeping claims about the amount of harm in healthcare either going up or down because we don't have an accurate benchmark or starting point to judge this. As Helen Hogan (2015) states in her recent article, 'The Problem with Preventable Deaths' in the *BMJ Quality and Safety*, there are significant limitations to measuring mortality as a way to show improved safety, as follows:

- Death is an uncommon outcome for many specialties, including obstetrics, psychiatry and surgical specialties such as ophthalmology, so relatively small numbers of deaths mean that random variation can have a large influence on trend data and it is unlikely to be an indicator of whether the specialty is safer or not.
- Nearly a quarter of all NHS hospital admissions are aged over 75 years and more than 40% of deaths occur in those older than 80 years, so half the UK population end their lives in hospital (with variation between hospitals, depending upon the provision of end-of-life care) and preventability of death is often difficult to determine.
- The vast majority of deaths do not involve safety problems. Even when errors of commission or omission do occur, establishing the degree to which healthcare has contributed to death among very elderly, frail patients with serious illness and multiple comorbidities towards the end of their natural lifespan and with just days or hours to live is difficult.

Rather than simply trying to count and attribute the number of deaths to avoidable harm, researchers recommended that reviews of individual deaths should focus on identifying ways of improving the quality and safety of care. Hogan (2015) suggests we should all focus on the major causes of preventable healthcare-related harm that we know about, for example, deaths associated with venous thromboembolism, surgical complications or hospital-acquired infections or falls as an alternative approach. She also suggests combining outcome with process measures to increase specificity when identifying preventable deaths, for example, measuring pulmonary embolism in patients who die and who did not receive adequate venous thromboembolism measures. She also believes that mortality statistics should not be used as an indicator of the safety of a hospital or any other healthcare facility, and says it is potentially misleading to praise or condemn a hospital on the basis of measuring mortality rates (Hogan et al. 2015).

In summary, none of the approaches described here truly take into account the complexity of healthcare, and most are focused on in-hospital care rather than across the whole healthcare system from acute care through to the patients' homes. Still, whether we agree or disagree on the scale of the harm, there is no doubt that patients are being harmed unnecessarily.

## Suggested Reading

*Practical Patient Safety*, written by John Reynard, John Reynolds and Peter Stevenson (published by Oxford University Press in 2009), provides further detail on the scale and nature of the problem together with some really good case studies of particular areas of harm.

# Chapter 3

---

# A Culture of Learning

---

The most important single change in the NHS …
would be for it to become, more than ever before, a
system devoted to continual learning and improvement of patient care, top to bottom and end to end.

**Don Berwick**
*2013*

## Are We Learning from Harm?

A culture of continuous learning was one of the key recommendations by Don Berwick (2013) for improving patient
safety across the National Health Service (NHS) in the UK.
Since the year 2000, there have been some notable improvements, for example in reducing particular healthcare-acquired
infections (Pronovost et al. 2008a, 2015). But in many other
respects, it is difficult to conclude that sustained changes have
been made to reduce areas of avoidable harm. The mystery
that motivates most of us who work in patient safety is why,
after more than two decade's worth of energy and resources
devoted to patient safety, progress has been so slow. The following three contrasting stories, one related to Johns Hopkins

Hospital in Baltimore, United States, another concerned with the care of Sam Morrish and his family in the NHS, UK and my own personal story, all demonstrate different approaches to learning from harm.

## Learning the Johns Hopkins Way

In 2001, two cases changed the future of Johns Hopkins Medicine. Early in the year, a young child, Josie King, died at Johns Hopkins Hospital in Baltimore, United States. She had been admitted with second-degree burns on more than half of her body after climbing into a bath full of hot water. After admission, she had begun to recover, when she developed sepsis and her condition deteriorated. She died of septic shock, just days before she was scheduled to return home.

Instead of seeing this as 'one of those things', the hospital wanted to learn from Josie's death and so set about investigating exactly what had happened and why she died. Unprecedented at the time, the hospital involved the family. They went to their home, apologised for her death and told them they would tell them everything they knew when they knew it. They were communicated with every Friday morning, even when there was little to report.

The investigations into Josie's death found that she had died of dehydration as a result of sepsis, a hospital-acquired infection. Similar to most patient safety incidents, there was much more to why Josie died than the care she received. Communications had failed, and importantly, Josie's parents were not listened to. Josie's parent's repeatedly told staff that their daughter was thirsty but these pleas were ignored.

In June of that year (2001), a 24-year-old woman, Ellen Roche, died of lung failure after inhaling an irritant medication while participating in an asthma research study. Ellen Roche was a technician in the Asthma and Allergy Center at

Johns Hopkins Bayview Medical Center and she had volunteered for an asthma study that would measure how healthy lungs respond to a chemical irritant, hexamethonium. She had participated in other studies previously, and was the third research subject. She was admitted to intensive care the day after she inhaled the chemical and died less than a month later.

These two deaths propelled the hospital to what some consider the most significant culture change in its history (Nitkin and Broadhead 2016). Fifteen years later, Johns Hopkins Medicine has pioneered a culture of accountability and advanced the field of patient safety science. Safety had become their top priority, with research oversight more rigorous. Research is carried out in settings that have been built around safety with each research team being taught how to handle an emergency. The hospital also employed a human factors engineer to study the interaction between clinicians and medical devices to improve their design and usability.

Peter Pronovost, one of the clinicians who worked at the children's unit where Josie died, viewed these events as a moral dilemma. The hospital had to make a choice: were they going to be open and admit their mistakes or were they going to chalk it up to 'one of those things' and move on. They decided to start talking.

Josie's parents channelled their grief into action. For example Josie's mother, Sorrel, wrote a book in 2009, *Josie's Story*, which is both a memoir and a call to action. She created the Josie King Foundation and the Josie King Hero Award for caregivers who create a culture of safety and gave the first one to Peter Pronovost. Fifteen years after her daughter's death, Sorrel King offers this advice to everyone involved in patient care: *'Slow down and take your eyes off the computer. Look at the patient in the bed and listen. Listen to that mother who is saying something is wrong'* (Nitkin and Broadhead 2016).

Johns Hopkins began treating safety like a science, collecting data to find, test and deploy systemic improvements. One of these related to bloodstream infections acquired through central-line catheters. Following Josie's death, Pronovost and his infection control colleagues distilled 120 pages of information from the Centers for Disease Control and Prevention into a five-step checklist. They looked at making things as easy as they could. For example, moveable carts were created with all the tubes, drapes and other equipment necessary for insertions so that doctors and nurses would no longer have to search for items in eight separate locations. The key step was to empower nurses to act and to speak up if they saw doctors skipping items on the checklist.

This was a major culture shift, which was embraced by top leadership but resisted by some physicians who did not like being told what to do by a nurse (Nitkin and Broadhead 2016). The work by Pronovost and his colleagues spoke for itself – it significantly reduced the numbers of infections and deaths in intensive care (Pronovost et al. 2008a). This work led to the creation of the Comprehensive Unit-based Safety Program (CUSP) at Johns Hopkins to address problems such as hospital-acquired infections, medication administration errors or communication breakdowns. With CUSP teams and checklists in 1100 intensive care units (ICUs) in 44 US states, bloodstream infections are down by 40% in those hospitals (Nitkin and Broadhead 2016).

Peter Pronovost is now a leading expert in patient safety (Pronovost et al. 2008b, 2011). He is also the director of the Armstrong Institute for Patient Safety and Quality. The Armstrong Institute, founded in 2011, leads patient safety work while at the same time training a new generation of patient safety champions. Clinicians receive emotional support when things go wrong. Family members are encouraged to assist with care and speak up if something doesn't look right. Improving patient safety isn't a choice at Johns Hopkins, it is an obligation (Nitkin and Broadhead 2016).

# Impact on Patients and Their Families: Sam's Story

There is a need for a cultural change that requires partnership between clinicians and patients (and their families) and a shared commitment to find, implement and evaluate solutions. The observations, memories and knowledge exist, but are divided between patients and staff. Insight and clear thinking, therefore, depend upon pooling that knowledge openly in order to allow a complete picture that can then be scrutinised in search of learning and the hope of reduced harm, increased patient safety and staff welfare (Morrish 2015).

This means being open with patients and the public, saying sorry, explaining the actions taken and providing assurance that lessons will be learned. NHS organisations need to demonstrate the right balance between positive support, fairness accountability and openness. But we make it really hard for the patients and the families involved who simply want answers. We make it really hard for clinicians to have a conversation with patients, one human to another.

The most important aspect of creating the right culture is to learn to listen. To patients and the people who care for them, listening is a vital skill and could be the difference between getting it right and getting it wrong. The patient, or the person who accompanies them, knows their own story – they may not know the answers but they know how they feel. Listen to the mums, the daughters, the husbands and the patients themselves. If they are worried or question an action, listen. Don't be too proud and too late. Make patients and colleagues feel their voice is worth listening to.

A heartbreaking example of a system failure and not learning from harm is found in the UK Parliamentary and Health Service Ombudsman (PHSO 2016) report on the death of a young, 3-year-old boy called Sam Morrish. Sam died from sepsis in December 2010. An investigation in 2014 found that, had Sam received appropriate care and treatment, he would have survived. However, this investigation failed to provide clear answers as to why Sam died.

Sam's parents therefore asked the Ombudsman to undertake a second investigation to find out why the NHS was unable to give them the answers they deserved after the tragic death of their son. The second investigation found a failing system. The catalogue of errors and incidents were many but they were not picked up through an investigation process that was not fit for purpose. The investigations carried out were not sufficiently independent, inquisitive, open or transparent. They were not properly focused on learning or able to span organisational and hierarchical barriers, and they excluded the family and many staff in the process. The Ombudsman concluded that, had the investigations been proper at the start, it may not have been necessary for the family to pursue a complaint. Sam's family should have been provided with clear and honest answers to their questions at the very outset.

The PHSO called for the NHS to build a culture that gives staff and organisations the confidence to find out if and why something went wrong and, importantly, learn from it. The PHSO called for investigations to be carried out thoroughly, transparently and fairly by the NHS in order to make service improvements possible. The PHSO called for a shift towards a more positive culture to drive both the development and embedding of organisational competence to investigate, learn and improve, and the confidence to challenge the lack of it. Indeed, this is also what Sam's family sought at every step of the journey but failed to achieve.

The PHSO report is of a collection of organisations and individuals who did not work together and failed to undertake effective individual investigations. Opportunities to learn were missed from the beginning and people were not adequately supported in their investigatory roles. Sadly, the failings identified in Sam's case are not isolated. Across the NHS, a fear of blame pervades that prevents individuals, staff and patients from speaking out.

The report is worth reading by anyone who works in healthcare, as it provides a summary of how poor a system can get. It should be used to review every aspect of the way we deliver healthcare to shift from a culture of judgment, fear and shame to one of compassion, learning and improvement. To shift away from a culture that perceives patients who die as unlucky and the bereaved as a problem to be managed to one that wants to learn from every patient death and one that involves the bereaved in every aspect of the investigation.

The lessons from the case can also be used as a blueprint to guide those who work in risk management, those who are tasked with investigating incidents and those who work in patient safety. There is a vital need for timely, objective and expert-led, learning-focused investigations that are conducted by skilled investigators.

Sam's family trusted the NHS and trusted those who work in it to find out what had happened and why; this should be at the very heart of any investigation. This includes informing the family from the outset and assigning someone to answer every single question they have and follow them up at regular intervals. It should never be left to patients or grieving families to drive the process for learning.

Scott Morrish (2015) also provided evidence to the Public Administration and Constitutional Affairs Committee (PASC 2015) in its review of NHS complaints and clinical failure. It is painful when you read his words:

> I don't believe the NHS was intentionally heartless or cruel, although at times it felt like it was both.

He went on to say

Patients who ask questions can be perceived as
a threat, especially if those questions might draw
attention to the NHS's own part in clinical failure or
untoward clinical incidents. This can even happen
when, as in my case, the motivation was purely a
need for understanding, and awareness (on my part)
of the possibility of learning. I was grieving, but consistently articulating no interest in blame. The NHS's
instinctive and, in human terms, rational response
to perceived threat is to retreat and defend itself, its
employees, and organisations - giving rise to a bun-
ker-mentality that allows the protection of reputations
to take precedence over the best interests of patients
or staff. Feeling embattled, apparently crippled by
fear, and preoccupied with itself, the NHS can lose
sight of patients – allowing them to be marginalised;
driving an ever-deeper wedge between patients and
staff; generating frustration, anger and yet-more-fear;
all of which can be intensified by adversarial complaints systems. It keeps defence unions, lawyers and
litigation authorities busy. For the rest of us it is painful, and costly. It tests character to the limit.

In the meantime patients and staff can find themselves isolated, in a no-man's land, their concerns
ignored, whilst everyone cedes responsibility to 'processes' and 'systems' without taking responsibility for
either. When no one feels responsible, everyone feels
powerless. Actions taken, decisions made and conclusions drawn, if inept, create more frustration, fear
and sometimes irreconcilable differences. It also leads
eventually to the despairing and fatalistic acceptance
of avoidable harm; the notion that there is no need
or point in investigation: there is no expectation of
learning. It gives rise to a universal feeling of pow-
erlessness where patients do not think it is worth
the phenomenal risks involved in raising concerns,

because staff seem (and feel) powerless to help; complaints handlers only find fault in systems, processes and services; and no one is deemed responsible for anything. When responsibility is ceded to large and complex processes and systems but no one takes responsibility for them: no one is accountable. This is not a figment of complainants imaginations.

The consequences are profound, insidious and pervasive to the point where they undermine the NHS by alienating patients from staff, and staff from each other, all the time eroding trust and respect in all directions. The same alienation and erosion of trust and respect occurs between commissioners and providers, and between both with their regulators. Nothing is learnt. Nothing changes.

It takes time, effort and determination, to understand all of this, but as the picture becomes more complete, it is no longer a mystery, or even a surprise that people we know to be kind, caring and good, can do or say apparently senseless things which, unintentionally, can cause additional suffering. The only way I can understand such paradoxical behaviour is in terms of culture, which can be paraphrased along the lines of 'Blame the system. It is not our fault. It is the way we do things around here'.

# Failing to Learn: My Own Story

After my general training, I first specialised in paediatrics and then paediatric intensive care. I worked on a unit in London, UK, which cared for patients with a range of illness. Children were sent to us from all over the country, sick with flu, asthma or other infections, or many who had been in accidents: falls, car crashes and house fires. We also had children following surgery and needing to recover for a few days so that they could be carefully monitored. These children were extremely ill and sometimes it took two nurses to provide the care that they needed. They were joined to multiple machines, multiple wires and pumps delivering the vital medications that were keeping them alive. The best part of working in paediatric intensive care was the reward of seeing a very sick child, not only get better, but come back to visit us. The worst part of the job was the children who did not survive.

To support the nurses at the bedside, there would be a leader, someone in charge of the whole unit who would make the shift run smoothly. The leader takes all the calls and attends the rounds with the doctors, seeing every patient and making sure that their nurses know what needs to be done. They are an expert resource, a counsellor and a coordinator. The leader is the central individual who everyone brings issues to, if something is broken or there is a need for a piece of equipment, or a family is upset or there are results to be delivered, and so on. This role is a problem-solver of any issues; no matter what comes up, the leader tries to figure out the answer or find someone who might know the answer. The leader does everything that is needed to ensure that the nurse by the child can concentrate all their efforts on looking after that child for the shift.

The hours were long; we did 12-hour shifts and, like all healthcare workers, we worked weekends and nights. Our shifts were split to around half the time day shifts and half the time night shifts. One of these night shifts started out as nothing out of the ordinary. I was a staff nurse and the designated nurse in charge. I had carried out this role many times before and I was a skilled paediatric intensive care nurse. A typical night was not that much different to a day and included multiple interruptions: telephone calls, visiting families, visiting doctors and questions from the team. This particular set of nights was very busy, but again this was not unusual. With only a few hours' sleep, I was exhausted; despite many years of practice, I was particularly bad at sleeping on night duty.

A number of our tasks had become very routine, and one of these was the drug rounds. These usually took over an hour as each child had multiple medications via multiple routes to be calculated and administered. Each child would have an array of syringes, some for the tube in their nose, some for the cannula in their veins and some to be put up as infusions to last a few hours. Our routine at the time was for the bedside nurse to draw up all of the drugs and for the nurse in charge to be the independent checker of the drugs that were sitting in a beige cardboard box. So I moved from bed to bed and checked the medications due for each child. The 10 p.m. medication round was no different to any other, or so I thought, and it would have been completed as usual at around 11 p.m.

Shortly after the medication round, a group of doctors arrived on the unit for the night round to check each patient to ensure that they were stable enough for them to perhaps get a few hours' sleep while we continued with their care. One of the doctors took me aside and asked about the syringe pump that was administering an antiviral drug to one of the children. He said that he thought it didn't look right. The particular antiviral drug was yellow in colour and being administered in a 50 ml syringe via an infusion pump by the child's bed. He said that the colour didn't look right, that it looked too yellow. The bedside nurse and I talked through with him what we had done and we quickly started to realise that we had drawn up the wrong dose. We had drawn up ten times the prescribed dose.

In that moment everything stood still. I can't recall how long I stood there but I do recall thinking I must move from this spot and sort this out. It was probably only a few seconds, but it felt like hours. I felt sick; I was mortified, deeply embarrassed and very frightened. What on earth had I done? I blamed myself completely. I should have paid more attention. I should not have been distracted. I should have checked the drug details more thoroughly. I thought I was infallible, dependable, unfailing, a perfect nurse who never made a mistake and here I was, someone who had put a vulnerable child at serious risk of harm.

The team quickly removed the infusion. It had not been up for that long, they kept saying to me; we are sure it will be fine, they reiterated time and time again to my ashen face. The child was monitored closely, bloods were taken for toxicity, vital signs checked for any indication of deterioration or change. To our relief, nothing untoward happened that night and there was no lasting impact from the drug overdose.

As part of our protocol at the time, any medication errors were expected to be recorded on a form and the person in charge of the hospital was to be informed. In those days, we had 'night sisters'; senior nurses who would oversee sections of the hospital and who themselves reported to a senior night sister. I informed the night sister covering our unit and handed her the form. Towards the end of the night, she returned and asked us to stay behind at the end of the shift. We were told we would have to be seen by the 'director of nursing'. The end of the shift came and I was responsible for handing over the night to the day team. Much to my shame, I had to tell them all about the medication error and asked them to monitor the child carefully.

After handover, we waited and waited and waited. Four hours later, we were asked to go and see the 'senior nurse'. We were tired, emotional and desperate to go home. I remember every detail of that meeting. I recall standing in front of her desk, she sitting looking over the form and then looking up at me. 'I expected more of you', 'how on earth did this happen'? and 'I thought you were better than this', she said. She told me that a formal written letter would be placed in my personnel file and that if I committed another error, I would be suspended. If I committed a third error, I would be referred to my governing body, the Nursing and Midwifery Council. A third error meant that my ability to be a nurse would be called into question. She wasn't being particular vindictive – this was the way things were at the time and sadly can still be the case. After this, we went home to attempt to sleep and then return for the final night.

Over the coming months, everyone on the unit knew about the incident but no one spoke about it. The nurses who did have the courage to talk to me said that they knew the implications for their careers and the incident had reminded them of this. They were fearful, and some had even decided that if something like that happened to them they would try their hardest to hide it and not tell a soul. They were not bad people – they were just frightened and simply wanted to carry on nursing.

There is one key lesson from this story – there was simply no learning. There was a presumption that this was down to competence, or the lack of it. The incident happened because we were not good nurses and that we needed to do better in the future. There was no investigation, no review that may have detected why the error was made. The parents were not informed. There were no changes to anyone's practice or the practice of the unit – everything simply carried on as before. I didn't know at the time that I would devote the second half of my career to trying to change all of that.

## Suggested Reading

'A Promise to Learn – A Commitment to Act: Improving the Safety of Patients in England'. This is commonly known as the Berwick Report and was published in 2013. The report was in part to respond to the failures in the NHS in the UK that were highlighted by the care at a hospital in Mid Staffordshire. It is one of those reports that, the more you read, the more profound it gets. On the face of it, the content and recommendations don't feel particularly new but they are described in such an eloquent way that the reader cannot fail to be moved by them.

'Learning from Mistakes' is the investigation report by the PHSO into how the NHS failed to properly investigate the death of Sam Morrish. Published in July 2016, this is vital and – in my view – compulsory reading for anyone who works in the NHS, all of whom should ask 'could this happen in my organisation?'

# Chapter 4

# Systems Approach to Safety

All incentives should point in the same direction.
In the end, culture will trump rules, standards and
control strategies every single time, and achieving
a vastly safer health service will depend far more
on major cultural change than on a new regulatory
regime.

**Don Berwick**
*2013*

## Understanding the Basics of a Safer System

Healthcare is provided within a set of systems, either the
whole hospital, a complex interacting set of functions that
work together to treat patients or the larger healthcare system
such as the National Health Service (NHS). The NHS is a set of
sub-systems that make up an entire system of healthcare that
includes a patient's home, community-based functions such
as health visitors or general practitioners, as well as specific
and specialist functions such as hospitals. It is not one single

system but a set of systems ranging from the ultra-safe to the ultra-adaptive (Vincent and Amalberti 2016).

The system is designed for better or worse, and that design helps or hinders the behaviour and performance of the individuals who work within it: the clinicians, the managers, the administrators and so on (Dekker and Leveson 2014). With respect to patient safety, incidents happen across the system as a result of a variety of factors and pressures that increase the risk at certain points. In fact, rather than incidents being a chance occurrence, they tend to involve a migration from safe care to unsafe care over time (Leveson 2012, Vincent and Amalberti 2016). Avoidable patient harm is in part attributed to a diverse spectrum of error-producing conditions across the system such as

- Human factors: Variation in training, individual experience, fatigue, boredom, depression and burnout
- Diversity of patients: Variation in age, severity of illness and comorbidities
- Working hours: Types of shift patterns and length of working hours
- Complicated technologies: Equipment, tasks and procedures
- Drugs: Calculations, drug names that look and sound alike, prescriptions, computerised prescribing and alert systems
- Design: Poor packaging, poor labelling and design of equipment
- Length of stay: Prolonged or multiple transfers
- Poor communication, handover, transitions and information

A safer system is one that is able to adapt and able to help the people who work within it adapt to their environment or to changes in their environment (Rasmussen 1990). A healthcare system designed around patient safety is more effective and efficient and significantly safer. The goal is not to limit human behaviour into a set of tasks but to design a system in which a human can function safely and effectively while at the same time being able to use their judgment and ingenuity.

## Learning from Other High-Risk Industries

Those who work in patient safety have also looked to other high-risk industries, such as the aviation and the nuclear industry, to learn about concepts like high-reliability organisations, LEAN methodology and resilience engineering. Comparisons and parallels between aviation safety systems and healthcare systems have been frequently made. Aviation is considered to have a much better record on safety than healthcare. There is no doubt that the aviation industry has an impressive safety record, which appears to be getting better all the time. These results have been achieved through a systematic and sustained focus on safety as a mindset rather than a simple set of tasks. It has also been achieved through a constant search for safer ways to design and fly airplanes. This comparison has led to policy makers and patient safety specialists focusing on establishing aviation type interventions such as incident reporting systems as a key priority.

One of the powerful aspects of the aviation safety system is the ability for those in aviation to work in partnership across the total worldwide aviation system. Over the last few years, they have been able to agree to the top seven safety priorities that have been key to the system's success. Organisations that, on the one hand, compete on a daily basis have all agreed to come together around a common purpose, to save lives, creating collective governance.

To have a common focus to agree on the safety outcomes that matter, create a supportive culture of continuous improvement and ensure that day-to-day risk controls are effective are all aspects that healthcare dreams of. Clarity about what a good culture looks like and then relentlessly pursuing that should be the focus of the healthcare industry over the next two decades. If aviation can do this, why can't healthcare across the globe come together around a common purpose: to save lives and agree on the things we should all focus on. If we did this, what would our top seven areas of risk be?

## Resilience

Concepts such as risk resilience (Macrae 2014a) have been embraced by these industries and are starting to be picked up by healthcare. Resilience is defined as the organisation's capacity to protect people from minor mishaps developing into major breakdowns. In simple terms, resilience is preventing minor things from getting worse or the minor incident becoming a catastrophe. The efforts are not in focusing on error and failure but on how safety can be maintained. Experts in this field talk of understanding what it means to have levels of acceptable risk, reduced risk resilience and degraded risk resilience (Hollnagel et al. 2006, Macrae 2014):

- *Acceptable* is as close as you can get an organisation to a safer system.
- *Reduced* is when processes for preventing or addressing risks are not as effective as they could be.
- *Degraded* is when there are few or no systematic defences so that the error turns into something far worse.

A resilient system is one that continually revises its approach to work in an effort to prevent or minimise failure, be constantly aware of the potential for failure and help people make decisions and direct (the limited) resources to minimise the risk of harm, knowing that the system is compromised because it includes sometimes faulty equipment, imperfect processes and fallible human beings (Amalberti

2005). Hollnagel and colleagues describe three key elements as part of resilience:

- Foresight or the ability to predict something bad happening
- Coping or the ability to prevent something bad from becoming worse
- Recovery or the ability to recover from something bad once it has happened

A resilient organisation is one whose workers are supported in these key elements so that safety is promoted by anticipating failure, by learning how to adapt to circumstances where failure is indicated and by restoring safe conditions after events. More recently, the field of patient safety is moving from the too-simplistic approach of capturing incidents and looking at them when we get it wrong to learning from when we get it right (Vincent 2004, Hollnagel et al. 2006, Jeffcott et al. 2009). This offers a proactive and positive system-based approach, allowing an organisation to understand both what sustains and what erodes its ability to adapt to changing pressures; that is, how to learn to stay 'safe' rather than focusing on error as an end in itself. It is innovative in that it looks proactively rather than reactively and does not assume that erratic people degrade an otherwise safe system. Instead, resilience aligns with what is described as a 'new view of human error' that sees humans in a system as a primary source of resilience in creating safety. The 'old view' focuses more on the elimination of risk rather than more realistically describing strategies that will circumscribe, cope and contain failure, as proposed by resilience.

## Safety I and Safety II

Eric Hollnagel (2014) has also introduced us to the concepts of Safety I and Safety II. In Safety I, the basic assumption is that the system is safe and that people make it unsafe. This is the current approach to safety, which is trying to ensure that only as few things as possible will go wrong and is a reactive approach to safety. In Safety II, we are much more proactive and interested in how things go right, how people are continuously trying to anticipate the potential for harm. Instead of humans being seen as a liability, in Safety II the systems are considered unsafe and the people create safety; humans are seen as a necessary component of system flexibility and resilience.

Hollnagel describes Safety I as a condition where as little as possible goes wrong and Safety II as a condition where as much as possible goes right. The pursuit is one of building a system where everything goes right. It is also the ability to succeed under unexpected conditions so that the number of intended actions and acceptable outcomes is as high as possible. This leads to the patient safety reviewer to find out how or why things go right and to ask how we can see what goes right. Hollnagel goes on to say that adopting a Safety II perspective does not mean that everything must be done differently or that current methods must be replaced wholesale. His recommendation is that we look at what is being done in a different way. It is still necessary to investigate things that go wrong and to consider the risks, but that when doing an investigation: adopt a different mindset. Safety I and Safety II are therefore complementary rather than incompatible or conflicting. We are only just at the beginning of understanding how important this different approach to safety is. Looking at the ways in which we get things right and learning to replicate this is now being seen as a vital step forward to creating an approach to safety which could final take us from a retrospective approach to a proactive approach to safety.

## Standardisation

In Patient safety and the problem of many hands (Dixon-Woods and Pronovost 2016), the authors reiterate the view held in this book, that healthcare worldwide is faced with a crisis of patient safety and that, despite huge optimism, effort, investment and some successes over the past 15 years or more, progress has been far too slow.

Dixon-Woods and Pronovost suggest that current strategies of leaving patient safety to individual organisations to sort out could be one of the problems, and that too many individuals are starting from scratch and wasting valuable resources and time.

Dixon-Woods and Pronovost argue for standardisation across systems to reduce the wasted time and energy of individuals inventing solutions and creating their own tools rather than adopting and adapting generic tools or solutions developed by others. For example, they point out the unintended consequences of creating local solutions such as different coloured allergy bands or labelling for drugs. When these are different from one hospital to another, then those that move around – in particular doctors – could be confused and are even set up to fail as a result. The visual clues in one hospital that make it safe can in another hospital make it unsafe.

## Human Factors

Additional concepts that have increased over the last 15 years include the integration of human factors and ergonomics within healthcare and patient safety (Jeffcott 2009, Catchpole 2013, Waterson and Catchpole 2015, Hignett et al. 2015). There are multiple human factors that are affected by the system that can also impact on the performance of the system, including mental workload, fatigue, boredom, distractions, the physical environment, device design, teamwork and the use of professional language such as acronyms and abbreviations (Jeffcott 2009).

However, these have yet to be embedded into daily activity. Waterson and Catchpole (2015) provide an excellent summary of the gaps in knowledge and the underexploited aspects of human factors that healthcare and patient safety could benefit from, including alternative ways to record and investigate incidents, the use of different methods to provide deeper insights into how safety is achieved and how it can fail and the application of socio-technical principles of design to reduce error-producing conditions.

For too long, we have focused on problems in isolation, one harm at a time. Our efforts have been simplistic and myopic (Darzi 2015). Across the UK, there are people who concentrate on falls, pressure ulcers, sepsis, acute kidney injury, or venous thromboembolism (VTE) ... the list goes on. These individuals are passionate about their particular area and can be lone individuals or groups, either inside or outside the organisation. They 'lobby' people for attention. What these individuals tend to do is focus others around them on reducing or eliminating specific harms through a project-by-project approach. Sadly, this approach does not appear to have led to widespread, holistic change. What it has done is create competing priorities. People are confused; they don't know which 'interest' or area of harm deserves more or less effort, time and resources. The system approach steers us to adopt a holistic, systematic approach that extends across cultural, technological and procedural boundaries.

Patient safety therefore requires concentration on the factors that thread throughout all of the individual areas of harm; a common set of causal or contributory factors such as communication, patient identification, patient observations, the sharing of information with each other and patients, the deficiencies in teamwork and team culture and the way we design the system and care pathway. These are the same cross-cutting or causal factors that happen time and time again and that have been found to explain the majority of the reasons why harm happens.

The system approach argued by Reason (1990), Dekker (2014) and others (NPSA 2004, Vincent and Amalberti 2016) supports the case that poor design or imperfect systems are to blame for patient harm and not the individuals who work in them. In addition to the relentless focus on these cross-cutting or common human factors, healthcare needs to invest in designers and develop procurement policies that support – where possible – standardisation of equipment and care processes. This will help us move from punishing individuals for errors to implementing safety systems in healthcare organisations to ensure safer practices.

## Shifting from 'One Size Fits All' to an Intelligent Approach to Risk

The concepts described here move us away from the predominant approach of the last two decades, none more so than that described in *Safer Healthcare* by Charles Vincent and Rene Amalberti (2016) to help create a more systematic approach to risk and patient safety and provide five different strategies for the spectrum of healthcare environments from the ultra-adaptive (such as accident and emergency or general practice) to the ultra-safe (such as radiotherapy). They add significantly to our knowledge in relation to looking at safety systems through the patient's eyes and looking at safety beyond hospitals, into primary care and into the patient's home. They also provide a compendium of safety strategies and interventions that readers can use as a checklist. Vincent and Amalberti (2016) also move our thinking on from a 'one-size-fits-all' approach to a multi-strategic approach to patient safety and risk management. This thoughtful book describes a continuum of care and safety. To the patient, it is never a nice neat line of consultation, admission and treatment, and it is rarely a single incident – it is usually a culmination of a number of small incidents, errors and mistakes along their healthcare journey and we need to learn about patient safety in the same way.

## Suggested Reading

*Human Error*, written by James Reason and first published in 1990. This book provides an in-depth description of the nature of error, error types, the detection of error and latent error conditions. It offers essential knowledge for anyone working in patient safety who truly wants to understand why human beings make mistakes.

*Resilience Engineering: Concepts and Precepts*, edited by Erik Hollnagel, David Woods and Nancy Leveson and published in 2006 by Ashgate offers the reader anything he or she could possibly want to know about resilience.

*Safer Healthcare Strategies for the Real World*, written by Charles Vincent and Rene Amalberti in 2016. Building on both Vincent and Amalberti's work in safety, this book provides new thinking on both patient safety and risk. It distils the learning from the past two decades into a short but highly informative book that provides the reader with a set of ideas, concepts and strategies that can be applied across the complex healthcare system, including the patient's home.

*Safety I and Safety II: The Past and Future of Safety Management* by Erik Hollnagel, published in 2014 by Ashgate, is a groundbreaking book that turns safety on its head. It eloquently provides the case for moving away from our current reactive approach to looking at safety in the negative and looking at safety in the positive. In doing so, it shifts us from studying error and harm to studying when we get it right.

# Chapter 5

# The Right Culture for Safety

Everyone needs to feel safe recognising and admitting mistakes in order for learning to be possible – especially when the consequences are catastrophic – that is where safety starts. If the focus was insight, learning and improvement rather than judgment, blame and shame – the NHS would flourish for patients and staff.

**Scott Morrish**

## The Just Culture

A safety culture is a set of shared values and norms that exist on two levels: above the surface – the behaviours of people who are aware they are being watched, and beneath the surface – the behaviours of people who are not being watched. A safety culture does not get built by a set of policies, goals, mission statements or job descriptions. These are superficial fixes that do not produce a shared set of values or behaviours. Equally, a culture of safety cannot be made by issuing a safety strategy document, placing safety notices on the walls or sending out alerts. A safety culture is even more than a mindset, it is a way of being.

The system approach is often misunderstood as the blame-free approach to patient safety. A fundamental component is a just culture: a culture that supports people when things go wrong and looks to understand why failures occur while at the same time ensuring that we take responsibility and are accountable for our actions. It is not a blame-free system; it is also not a polarisation of people or systems, it is people *in* systems, people *and* systems (Dekker and Leveson 2014). The just culture does not also ignore that there may be some individuals who are incompetent.

The prevailing view is that a small percentage of people are responsible for a large percentage of incidents and that by removing these people the system will become safer. There are others who view the fact that there are a few who are more error prone than others because they are working in complex, risky situations that create more error-producing conditions than others. However, the view is that incompetence is, in a large part, due to the system design not providing the relevant training, education, support, supervision and so on to ensure that the individual is as competent as they can be. There may be some individuals who are not suited to certain roles and if despite the level of support they remain incompetent, then robust processes should be in place to detect this quickly, to appraise the individual in their performance and, if necessary, help them find a role they are more suited to. This is neither blaming nor blame-free, it is the just culture for safety.

The default mode should be that if a clinician is erroneous then they should be supported and we should learn why they are erroneous. If they are following this review and are found to be incompetent, then they require support to increase or improve their performance: training, mentoring, supervision – not punishment. Only if the incompetence is not addressed by the individual or is judged as gross incompetence should we consider sanctions or punishment. This could include being referred to their regulatory body who can judge whether they should continue to practice, be suspended from practice or stopped altogether. The issue is not how we get rid of those who are incompetent but how did we create them in the first place? The solution is to improve the system that identifies and deals with incompetence.

In some cases, which appear to be completely arbitrary and random, clinicians are not referred to their professional body but referred to the criminal judiciary instead. These clinicians, who on the face of it did not appear to 'intend' to commit the error or action, are considered as having done so. The legal term 'reckless' is an intentional disregard for others' well-being. There have been a number of clinicians in the UK charged with manslaughter (Brahams 1991).

People who work in healthcare fundamentally want to do a great job and if we get the right culture where staff can feel supported when things go wrong and are able to speak out when they are concerned about safety, we will be able to learn about what we can do differently to make care safer. Somewhere out there is a doctor, nurse or other healthcare worker making a mistake now. They will need to be supported, helped to learn and supported to cope. Part of the recipe for success in creating the right culture is to care for those who care, and to put safety first we also need to put our staff first.

Over the years, individuals involved in incidents have not only tortured themselves, they have been punished for their actions by the people they work with and for. Some have also been suspended, sacked, lost their ability to perform their duties, removed from their professional body or even charged with manslaughter. The whole issue of poor performance versus criminal behaviour has been debated for years.

The right response is at the heart of the just culture and is vital for both the safety of patients and the well-being of all. Following the death of their son Sam, Scott and Sue Morrish could so easily have blamed. The striking thing about them is their ability to be compassionate and to care. They embody all of the traits all of us should have. They do so from a place of grief and loss. They have chosen not to blame when they were pushed from one organisation to another, when they were told not to pick a fight with the National Health Service (NHS). Their 'taking on the system' has created, in their words, tremendous levels of stress and anxiety. Yet, they can also say how grateful they are for people who continue to work in the NHS. That's compassionate leadership. The way we can honour them and Sam's memory is to reflect on the insight from the investigation report and, more importantly, turn the Parliamentary and Health Service Ombudsman (PHSO) report recommendations into reality (PHSO 2016).

Today, the description of a just culture has been refined to three areas: human error, risky behaviour and recklessness. In reality, it is not quite as simple as that implies. There are no neat lines between these three different behaviours, but they do provide us with a foundation on which to base our understanding of what a safety culture should include. At its core, the just culture community believes that blame is the enemy of safety (Marx 2009, Leveson 2012, Dekker 2012). Safety is reliant on people being able to speak up, not cover up. A resilient culture is where individuals within an organisation have a constant and active awareness of the potential for things to go wrong. A just culture is where individuals who notice these things can share information openly and freely about their concerns and are treated fairly when something goes wrong. With a culture that is at least 2500 years old, it is little surprise that changing the culture from stigmatising errors to being open about them is hard to do (Dekker 2012).

One of the best papers on patient safety and the just culture was published in 2001 by David Marx: 'Patient Safety and the Just Culture: A Primer for Health Care Executives'. Marx described the four behavioural concepts referred to above: human error, negligence conduct, violations and reckless conduct. There are a number of things that can be done today to build a just culture. Provide visible leadership of what is expected in terms of values and behaviours and support people when they make a mistake, and make this clear in all the relevant policies and procedures. Understand what response is required for the different components. The key issue is to ensure that learning from the events outweighs the deterrent effect of punishment and your staff feel able to speak out, raise concerns and report incidents.

> The single greatest impediment to error prevention is that we punish people for making mistakes.
>
> **Lucian Leape**
> *1997*

In simple terms, the response to the three different components of the just culture should be that

■ People who make an error (human error) are cared for and supported.
■ People who don't adhere to rules and policies (risky behaviour) are asked first before being judged.
■ People who intentionally put their patients or themselves at risk (reckless behaviour) are held accountable for their actions and should be disciplined.

## Human Error

Human error happens when healthcare workers are going about their day-to-day tasks; they occur when they are bored and when they are busy, when they are pressured and when they are not. We are now aware of how stress, distractions, being unfocused, being too busy or not being busy enough can all lead to an increased propensity for error. In fact, those who have erred are more likely to do it again because of the stress caused by the first error. Crucially, we have learnt that we will never eliminate human error, so we need to create a culture whereby we aim to minimise the chances or the impact of error as much as we can. We are slowly moving away from focusing purely on the individual at the end of the incident. There is an increasing number of people who accept that people make mistakes and that there are processes that can prevent people from making those mistakes.

## Risky Behaviour

Negligence, says Marx, is subjectively more culpable than human error. Negligence, as a legal term, revolves around 'duty of care', 'breach of the duty of care' and 'impact of the breach in relation to the injured party'. In healthcare, this means assessing whether there was a duty to provide a standard of care, that when something went wrong was it a breach of that duty and, if so, did it result in injury or harm. Negligence is the failure to recognise a risk that should have been recognised.

Violations, says Marx, happen when healthcare practitioners are faced with situations in which they may need to take a risk. These are often referred to as violations that are defined as when individuals or groups take action that is different from the expected standard or rules or procedures. There are a number of different types of violations:

- Erroneous: The clinician did not fully understand the policy and was not aware of the right steps to take.
- Routine: It is routine to move patients around the hospital when other parts are full or busy.
- Situational or exceptional: The clinician changes the normal procedure for a patient.
- Optimising: It appeared to be better to do the procedure in a different way.
- Unintentional: The clinician did not intend to do the wrong thing.

The words violating or violation have strong connotations of 'disgraceful behaviour'; the tone is already set for those who are found to have not adhered to a set procedure for some reason or other. We don't have a clear understanding of the scale and nature of the problem of violations as incident reporting systems are poor at reflecting the nature and frequency of violations, especially in relation to routine violations as they become normal – the 'way we do things round here'. If regarded as usual practice (not necessarily the written practice), then they will not be detected until perhaps something serious happens.

Much can be learned by understanding why certain violations happen and why some become the norm, so the response required for risky behaviour is to pause before judging and to try to understand why. Ken Catchpole (2013) states: 'violations and non-adherence are common, not always conscious, not always planned, are frequently well meaning, and in many cases allow the system to run smoothly'. Understanding why people 'violate' policies and procedures is a key component of patient safety. The reasons may lead to valuable lessons for the organisation, who may need to rewrite some of the standards or rules or may have to consider how these rules could be made easier to implement.

Recent terminology has moved from violations to that of risky behaviour. In clinical risk, terms relate to the decisions and choices made that may increase risk. Most treatments come with a set of risks – risk of complications or side effects, for example. In discussions with patients, decisions are made as to whether the risk is justified or acceptable. We make it hard for people to get things right. Drug labels and equipment layouts lacking in standardisation and poor design lead individuals to make repetitive errors. We have learnt that, for all the obvious incidents or errors, there are likely to be many more subtle, wrong decisions that healthcare workers make every day and that are difficult to trace through a patient's care. In fact, errors can happen without the doctor or nurse knowing that they have made them.

## Reckless Behaviour

Reckless behaviour is often referred to as gross negligence, and involves a higher degree of culpability than negligence. It is a disregard by a healthcare practitioner of the risk to the patients, or to themselves or their colleagues. Recklessness is the conscious disregard of a visible and significant risk, such as reckless driving. Recklessness or reckless behaviour is greater than violations or negligence; it is an intentional disregard of the risks associated with a decision, choice or action. Examples are drink driving, driving at excessive speed, conducting a clinical treatment that you have no idea how to perform and have not been trained in, using new drugs or equipment without seeking help and so on. Consider that you are driving and you see a car ahead, both speeding and weaving in and out of lanes. The car is violating traffic rules and taking a risk that could cause an accident. It is highly likely that the driver knows the risk they are taking. The response required is for the individual to take responsibility for their actions and to be called to account. This is the extreme end of patient safety and is the only time when the individual requires discipline, sanction and punishment. This is why the just culture is not a blame-free culture.

One of the most extreme examples of recklessness is found in the story of flight 9525. On March 24, 2015, a pilot named Andreas Lubitz took off from Barcelona flying Germanwings flight 9525. The airplane was scheduled to land in Dusseldorf 2 hours later. But flight 9525 never made it to Germany. Andreas Lubitz deliberately crashed the Airbus into the French Alps, about 100 miles north-west of the coastal city of Nice. All 144 passengers and six crew members died.

The black box was found on the same day and slowly the investigators started to piece together what had happened. The flight left Barcelona at 9:35, rising over the city and banking gently towards the Mediterranean Sea. In the cockpit was Captain Patrick Sondenheimer and his co-pilot, Andreas

Lubitz. At one point, the black box revealed, Sondenheimer mentioned to Lubitz that he had not been to the bathroom before they boarded. Lubitz told him to 'go anytime'. Just under an hour into the flight, Sondenheimer did just that. What Sondenheimer didn't know was that Lubitz was suffering from depression and had had thoughts of suicide.

Lubitz had suffered depression from the early days of his training but had also lied at various points of his career about the extent of the problem, even at one point denying that he had ever been diagnosed as having a mental disorder. He joined Germanwings in late 2013. In 2014, he was known to have visited a number of ophthalmologists and neurologists, complaining of seeing flashes of light and double vision among other symptoms. It was considered by those he met that he was experiencing a psychological rather than a physical disorder. A few months later, his Internet search records suggest these suicidal thoughts, with searches related to 'drinking gasoline', 'poisons that kills without pain' and, chillingly, 'the locking mechanisms on an airbus A320 cockpit door'. On the outbound flight to Barcelona, the black box from that flight shows that while Sondenheimer was out of the cockpit, Lubitz briefly switched the plane's autopilot to 100 feet, appearing to undertake a test run for the return journey. This was brief and not noticed by any air traffic controllers.

On the doomed flight 9525, after Sondenheimer left, Lubitz immediately put his plan into action. He locked the cockpit door and disabled Sondenheimer's emergency access code. He switched the plane's autopilot to 100 feet and the plane began to drop at a rate of 3500 feet per minute. This was noticed by French air traffic controllers, who contacted the aircraft. Lubitz did not reply to their call. Three minutes later, Sondenheimer returned to the cockpit door, entered his code, but was denied access. He was heard to knock at the door, telling Lubitz to let him in. With no response, he starts to shout at Lubitz. He tries to smash the door in, still screaming at Lubitz to open the door. Lubitz is heard to be breathing calmly. Moments later the plane crashes into the mountain at just over 400 miles per hour.

This was no human error, but a mix of intentional violation of procedures and rules with a conscious and intentional disregard for his own life and for all of the people who were on board that fateful flight in March 2015. It is extraordinarily rare for a pilot to commit murder-suicide in the cockpit, and the best way to protect against a single person crashing a plane is to require every airplane to have two people in the cockpit at all times. This was already standard protocol in the United States, but not widespread in Europe. If a second person – a co-pilot or even an airline attendant – had been in the cockpit with Lubitz, he or she would have had an opportunity to intervene. Three days after the crash, Lufthansa issued a policy change requiring every one of their flights to have two pilots in the cockpit at all times. Other European airlines quickly followed suit, implementing a similar protocol. Not only is this an extreme example of recklessness, it is also an example of how airline investigations often result in policy changes for the entire aviation industry.

## Suggested Reading

*Just Culture*, written by Sidney Dekker and published in 2007 with a second edition in 2012. This book offers a detailed and fascinating look at just culture, not only in healthcare but across society.

*Whack-a-Mole: The Price We Pay For Expecting Perfection*, written by David Marx in 2009, also offers the reader insights into human error and human fallibility and what the right approach to mistakes should be.

## Chapter 6

# Learning or Counting from Incidents

We collect too much and do too little.

**Macrae**
*2015*

## Incident Reporting

As Erik Hollnagel says, the approaches we have taken to date in the field of patient safety have potentially become obsolete because while it has stayed the same, the world has changed. When something goes wrong, it is unlikely to be unique; it is more likely to be something that has gone well time and time again before and that on this one occasion, something failed. It is also likely that, even though it failed on this occasion, it will go well many times again in the future (Hollnagel 2014).

The 'easy to see' incidents are usually the ones that get reported via an incident reporting system. This is the traditional approach to collecting information from front-line staff, usually about an incident that has led to a patient being harmed. Other methods of identifying when things may or may not have gone wrong include the case note review methods referred to earlier. This is where an episode of care is reviewed to see if the care did or did not go to plan or led to a patient being harmed or an avoidable death. None of these methods are ideal and none of them capture all of the relevant safety information that could provide an estimation of the levels of safety in a department or organisation. There are also, as we have discussed, limited data related to out-of-hospital care settings even though patients who arrive in the emergency department are often there because of a patient safety incident that occurred in the community.

One autumn day in 2015, I came across a webinar titled Patient safety after 15 years: disappointments, successes, and what's on the horizon. This was a series on patient safety. Dr Kaveh Shojania set the context by providing an overview of the past 15 years of the patient safety movement from *To Err is Human* (Institute of Medicine 1999) to the current day. During the webinar, Shojania (2015) was talking about incident reporting when he said, '*incident reporting is the single biggest waste of time in the last fifteen years*'. This really intrigued me and I started to think about whether he was right.

Over time, incident reporting systems have become one of the most widespread safety strategies in healthcare, both within individual organisations and across entire healthcare systems (Macrae 2014a, 2014b, 2015). There is no doubt that incident reporting systems are a vital tool in the risk toolbox. Reporting systems that allow fast and translatable intelligence to be shared across the globe, and thereby prevent error, are common in aviation and other high-risk industries. Patients are dying, in part because people have not shared the information so that changes could be put in place to prevent future errors. Learning from one area of healthcare, one geographical area or even one country to another was precisely the intent behind the design of the UK national reporting and learning system (Donaldson 2004).

However, there are a significant number of problems with incident reporting systems.

Incident reporting systems, instead of being seen as useful insights into areas of risk or concern, are viewed as bureaucratic tools to performance-manage individuals, teams and entire organisations. The processes are too complicated – there is a lack of feedback, a lack of visible action; the process does not appear to drive change and has a general feeling of 'why bother'. It has remained a relatively passive process of individuals submitting reports to a central team who may or may not respond with feedback – information sharing rather than participative improvement.

The statement that Shojania made prompted me to reflect on the work I had been involved in at the National Patient Safety Agency (NPSA) in the UK, when we set up the National Reporting and Learning System (NRLS). Today, as I write, the NRLS currently captures over 1.3 million incidents a year. Even with this large number, it is considered that only around 5% of the incidents that happen are captured by this and other incident reporting systems (Sari et al. 2007a, 2007b, Hogan et al. 2012). To put these big data in context, the NHS in 2014–2015 dealt with over 1 million patients every 36 hours, saw 22.364 million people in the emergency departments, had 85.632 million outpatient attendances and managed 15.892 million total hospital admissions (NHS Confederation 2016). From a technological perspective, the NRLS is a successful system; with very few hitches, it continues to capture incidents from across England and Wales day in, day out. With hindsight, there should be recognition that an undertaking of this scale was a lot more complex than anybody had perhaps at first realised. When the system was set up, it was the first of its type in the world.

The NRLS was developed at the NPSA by a team of patient safety experts, analysts, information technology specialists and risk managers who came together to bring to life the desire to create a reporting system that would identify safety problems and use those problems to identify solutions for improvement across the NHS. There were disparate views across the team on the best approach. Some called for replicating the reporting processes and philosophies that have worked in aviation, others suggested replicating a system in Australia that had been set up to capture anaesthesia incidents and some suggested designing a bespoke system for the NHS. At the time, the majority of hospitals had a version of an incident reporting system but there was no unified approach.

The designers of the national system wanted to add value to these local systems but to not add any burden to already busy front-line or risk management staff. Where possible, it needed to be designed so that it did not duplicate other reporting activities or bypass the local system. The NPSA was provided advice from researchers who told the team that there would be no point in making the system mandatory and that it would be impossible to know if this requirement had been complied with. The NPSA therefore chose to set up a voluntary reporting system that was linked to and uploaded from systems in each hospital at the click of a button. The reports received were graded according to severity, from 'no harm' through to death. The definition for reporting to the NRLS was 'any unintended or unexpected incident that could have or did lead to harm'.

The national system should then aggregate all the individual system data, identify themes across the whole system and make recommendations that apply everywhere. A national taxonomy and data set was designed. The NPSA employed 33 patient safety managers who (among all their other duties) travelled the length and breadth of England and Wales helping individual risk managers to map their data sets to the national data set.

When the NPSA first set up the NRLS, it expected to receive a few hundred incident reports. Researchers had previously found that incident reporting systems rarely, if ever, capture the total number of incidents occurring and that there was a lack of trust among clinicians, mainly doctors, about what the receivers would do with the information. Therefore, the NPSA genuinely thought that people would be fearful of reporting through to a national organisation. In order to counter these risks, the NPSA carried out an awareness-raising campaign and encouraged people and organisations to report. The mantra was 'a good reporting culture demonstrates a good safety culture'.

To the NPSA's surprise, reports arrived in their thousands. At the time of writing this book, around 1.3 million reports are submitted each year – over 3500 a day and over 100,000 a month. The system has captured over 10 million incident reports since its inception, making it the largest patient safety database in the world. The current emphasis on more reports has overloaded the system, from the national database all the way through to front-line teams. Current reports are mainly related to the incidents that are important to nursing staff; doctors in particular mainly use different methods to capture and learn from when things go wrong.

# Learning from Incident Reporting

The most important aspect of safety is to learn about what we can do in the future. The best source of patient safety information is the people who actually do the work. However, the worst way of seeking this information is an incident reporting system. In the main, this learning should take place within the organisation or department to learn and put in place solutions or changes that are relevant for that individual organisation.

Incident reporting systems capture the same things month after month with very little new information. For example, patient falls are the highest-reported incident in the NRLS. This is because they are easy to see and almost always considered to be the 'fault of the patient' – the patient was confused and fell, or the patient tried to move unaided and fell. There are also incidents that are usually caused by poor design of equipment, furniture and ward design rather than the competence of the individual healthcare practitioners. Therefore, they are least likely to be used to blame an individual healthcare practitioner. All of these factors mean that they are 'easy to report'.

Shojania (2015) suggested that there is almost no point in reporting a fall and that they are a common enough problem at every hospital that it should stop doing incident reports. With so many falls happening, one would assume that there is a ton of learning that could be used to prevent them from ever happening again. However, we tend to simply count them and quantify and capture the number of falls. Incident reporting systems do this a lot: capture and count large numbers of the same types of incidents, which is great if all we want to do is count, but at some point we should aim to do more than count and instead learn. Simply continuing to capture does not seem to help with our learning.

Capturing the easy to report or the reports submitted by one profession has a knock-on effect to prioritising action and activities that may not be as important to address as other issues that only have a handful of reports to their name. At a national level, the numbers and types of incidents reported are then used to shape patient safety policy and create patient safety alerts and other national interventions. As for the mantra that repeated reports of the same type of event suggest a strong culture of reporting, what this actually means is that there is a poor culture of learning. Also, reduced reports of a particular type might simply indicate that people became accustomed to something happening, grew tired of reporting or stopped noticing the problem in question. Thus, when reports decline, incident data on their own cannot distinguish between a reassuring improvement in safety or a concerning organisational blind spot (Macrae 2015).

As Carl Macrae (2015) says in his article, 'The Problem with Incident Reporting', healthcare has nothing like the history of systematic investigation that aviation has. Instead, incident

reporting systems have focused on collecting and process-
ing large quantities of incident data. Macrae tells us that, in
1989, British Airways possessed 47 four-drawer filing cabinets
full of the results of past investigations, and that most of this
paperwork had only historic value. He says that an army of
personnel would have been required if the files were to be
comprehensively examined for trends or to produce useful
analyses. Sadly, he concludes that, rather than recreating the
organisational infrastructures that underpin routine investigation and coordinated inquiry in aviation, healthcare has simply reproduced the filing cabinets. This focus on the quantity
of incidents reported rather than the quality of investigation
and improvement activities has perpetuated a range of inter-
related problems. Instead of developing as a critical way in
which an organisation or a team can learn about failures in
healthcare, they have become simply a counting machine. The
original ambitions have been forgotten and now all people do
is collect the problems. There is little time to investigate and
address the problems or to share the resulting lessons. Macrae
sums it up for me when he says '*we collect too much and do
too little*'.

Both at a national and hospital level, teams are not set
up to analyse this many incident reports. Decisions have to
be made about how large data collections can be analysed
and how areas of risk can be identified and shared across an
organisation or across the NHS in order to prevent the same
thing from happening elsewhere. As a clinical risk manager, I all too clearly remember the relentless flow of paper
reports arriving on my desk. My day was filled with desperate attempts to keep up with inputting the reports into the
database and trying to analyse them to see what they were
telling me about the state of the organisation. As Macrae says,
all I was actually doing was counting them and I never really
felt I got on top of them. Incident reports were supposed to
help us fix things. However, I don't recall them helping me fix
things where I worked. I focused on pie charts and trend data

of what got reported and the numbers continued to rise year on year with consistently the same types of incidents reported from consistently the same settings and people.

At the NPSA, the only way the organisation coped with the amount of data was to set up a team of clinical reviewers to analyse only the incidents that were classified as 'serious harm' (permanent harm) or 'death'. In reviewing this subset of incidents, trends and themes could be identified and then used to data mine the rest of the database for similar incidents at different grades. The information gained was then used to issue alerts – notices to the NHS to be aware of a particular risk or to change practice. For example, early alerts raised awareness about the dangers of concentrated potassium chloride, the risks associated with the administration of methotrexate or the risks associated with nasogastric tube insertion.

## Performance Management

Incident reporting should not be used to performance-manage individuals or organisations. In the UK NRLS system, the incidents are counted and categorised and each individual organisation is rated according to its reporting rate. This is then published in a league table to help organisations benchmark themselves against similar organisations. This created some interesting and unexpected behaviours. The philosophy pressured organisations to increase reporting just for the sake of increasing the numbers. Those at the top of the list were deemed good reporters but were also at the same time worried that they looked like they were more erroneous than others on the list. Those in the middle, instead of using the list to ask themselves what they could do to improve reporting, were happy to remain in the middle. This was because they were left alone as a result. Those at the bottom of the list were used as examples of organisations that did not take safety seriously. These organisations were the ones that filled their reporting systems with operational issues to make it appear that their reporting was increasing. What we have created is a culture of mediocrity.

Macrae (2015) and others (NPSA 2004, 2005; Mitchell et al. 2016) suggest a number of reasons why incident reporting should not be used as a way of measuring safety in an organisation:

- Incident reporting systems have never captured all the things that go wrong on a day-to-day basis and only detect a tiny fraction of what is actually happening.
- The data are skewed. People are biased towards reporting particular types of incidents but not others. Incident reporting systems are used to capture problems better suited to other strategies. They are used as a kind of 'information system to talk to management', a way of airing grievances about resources or staffing levels. Nursing staff, in particular, use the reporting systems to share their frustration at all sorts of administrative issues that are not particularly safety related. While these may impact on safety, they end up by drowning out the important information – truly hiding the proverbial needle in the haystack.
- Very few doctors report patient safety incidents. Instead, incident reporting is largely undertaken by nurses and incident reporting systems largely fall under their governance units within healthcare organisations. Doctors' reluctance to report incidents appears to be multifactorial and includes time constraints, fear of reputation and an inability to show they have failed, as well as medico-legal fears.
- There is also a lack of clarity about what to report and a paucity of feedback regarding previously submitted reports together with a lack of solutions or answers that could prevent the incidents from happening again. Putting it simply, they are not helpful.
- The data captured are mainly high-frequency, low-grade incidents – again, easier to report.

## Quality of Reports

There is huge variation in the quality of information captured in incident reporting forms, whether they are electronic or paper based. The information is often sparse, badly worded and incorrect. The way to analyse incidents effectively is to use 'key word' searches. However, even this is impossible. In a recent review of the NRLS (Mayer et al. 2016), one of the findings was that reporters spell the same things in multiple ways. One of the most astonishing was that *Clostridium difficile* (a type of infection) was spelt 371 different ways in NRLS reports. This makes it very hard when you want to (as the analysts say) interrogate the data – putting in 371 key words for a search on incidents related to *Clostridium difficile* is somewhat tricky and time-consuming. This is also only one example – when free text is used in a reporting system, there will always be multiple ways in which a single issue can be described. The review also found that the data fields are rarely fully completed and the free text boxes range from single word submissions (e.g. one word such as 'fall' or two words such as 'drug error') to over 800-word narratives.

## The Truth

Incident reports are, in the main, based on one person's side of the story. When an incident occurs for reasons including emotion, stress, pressure or distraction, the truth will be hard to find. We all know, when telling stories about our own lives, that we sometimes miss things out, elaborate a fact to make a point or even truly believe that we saw something that in fact wasn't there. We know in any aspect of life that there are multiple versions of the truth and facts. For one person, there is their version of the truth, the facts, and the event and for another, there is a different version of the same incident. Incident reports begin with one person's partial view of a complex clinical and organisational situation. We know, for example, that when two people look at a painting, they will both walk away with different versions of what they saw. This is exactly the same for an incident. In medication safety, for example, individuals are often reported to say 'but I saw 100 mgs and gave 100 mgs, but when I look back at the chart I now see it as 10 mgs'. This natural behaviour is often referred to as the human factors that make us both safe and unsafe. So to see incident reports as telling the exact truth is wrong.

## What Can Be Done Differently for Incident Reporting?

Collecting relevant, useful and meaningful information through incident reporting systems is important. But the use of incident data needs to be understood in relation to their purpose. Is the information collected so that incidents can be counted? If so, this would require mandatory reporting of a standard set of incidents. If the information collected is for learning, then the incident reports should be used as a mechanism to trigger further review or investigation. For learning, the focus should change from reporting any and all incidents to focusing on serious or specific incidents. Methods to avoid swamping the systems should be used, such as triage processes or limiting the types of incidents reported.

In 2003, Denmark was the first country in the world to adopt a law that required healthcare practitioners who worked in hospitals to report patient safety incidents. Denmark created a national reporting system, which was made strictly confidential. In 2010 and 2011, the law was expanded to cover all of healthcare, including primary care, and to allow incident reporting from patients and their families. This system has also been subjected to scrutiny and criticism (Rabøl et al. 2016). The Danish system is considered too bureaucratic, with too little learning and too few actions from the 180,000 incidents reported each year. In January 2016, the Danish Society for Patient Safety brought together key stakeholders to create recommendations for the future of incident reporting (Rabøl 2016). They made eight recommendations, similar to those identified by Macrae (2015):

1. Only report incidents of importance, new or surprising events – events that have the potential for learning.
2. Reporting should be easy – it takes around 20–30 minutes to complete an incident report form and then it has to travel the length and breadth of the organisation's governance systems before action can be taken.
3. Disciplinary action should be clearly separated from incident reporting, which should be all about learning.
4. The 'levels' of reporting should be optimised, with local reporting to solve local issues and national reporting to solve national issues.
5. Learning must be shared across the system.
6. Incident reporting should be integrated with other components of safety (and quality).
7. Reporting should be transparent.
8. The reporter must receive individual feedback about actions taken.

The primary purpose of incident reporting should be to identify an underlying risk in the healthcare system and determine the need for further investigation and analysis. In fact, incident reports themselves do not need much detail. All they need is enough detail to trigger further action. The search for safety starts, rather than ends, with incident reports (Macrae 2015). Over the next two decades, we must refocus our efforts and develop more sophisticated and intelligent ways of capturing error and avoidable harm. We need better ways of learning from these data and better ways to share that learning (Macrae 2015).

One way may be to not use an incident report at all. Erik Hollnagel (2014) suggests that we interview people instead of completing forms. The goal of the interview would be to find out how people normally do their work and therefore how, in certain cases, it can deviate from this norm. Asking in-depth questions about how people work, their working conditions and their work situations, and finding out things that get in the way of working well as well as the pressures people face day to day will be significantly more insightful than a short incident report. This is a form of appreciative inquiry or co-operative inquiry or 'exnovation', which is where practitioners describe as far as possible what happened as they experienced it (Hollnagel 2014).

Often, clinicians say to me that the cause of an incident is already clear. It is with this mindset that we tested a structured debrief, an ideal example of a post-incident review. In 2015, rather than providing a lecture on learning from incidents for a small group of junior doctors, I chose to use a form of structured debrief. I provided a scenario of a medication error and asked them to sit quietly on their own for 5 minutes to consider why a child may have been administered ten times the dose of morphine. After 5 minutes, I asked them to talk to their neighbour about what they thought the contributory factors were. Again, this was for 5 minutes. The pairs were then asked to share their findings. In 10 minutes, they were all able to articulate the top ten reasons or contributory factors that would lead to a child receiving ten times the dose of a drug. We then went on to discuss what could be done to prevent that incident from happening again. The whole interaction lasted half an hour.

Compare the usual scenario of completing a form, sub-mitted the form through the governance structures of an organisation and waiting for months for some feedback and learning. Compare that with taking 30 minutes out of the day to truly learn about why things go wrong and what could be done differently. What's not to like?

# Chapter 7

# Relegated to the Back Office

Air Accidents Investigation Branch inspectors, usually airline pilots, are regarded in the industry as credible and trustworthy: it is a role that is seen by many as the pinnacle of their career.

**Graham Braithwaite**
*Cranfield University (PASC 2015)*

## Risk Management and Incident Investigation

Patient safety ranges from clinical risk management through to safety improvement. If we relegate clinical risk to the back office, we are in danger of missing a vital piece of the safety jigsaw. Those working in the field today would be surprised about how very little information or guidance there was to help those working in risk in the 1980s and 1990s. During this time, there was no Internet or Google to search for the latest thinking, nor was there access to training. Training was by experience – on the job, feeling our way from day to day. This was so different from when I trained as a nurse and then went on to specialise in the Paediatric Intensive Care Unit (PICU). Then, I was carefully taken from the role of a novice through to an expert with an in-depth training programme, supervision, mentorship, shadowing, coaching and tons of experiential learning. In fact, most roles in healthcare, whether they are clinical, managerial or administrative, have access to training programmes and support mechanisms that provide them with the requirements to do the job.

Sadly, even today as I write this, there is very little to support the role of a clinical risk manager or patient safety manager. Learning is still down to the individual and often achieved through attending one- or two-day conferences a year. There are some courses that people can attend, but these are limited in number. It is not surprising, therefore, to find huge variations in skills and expertise across healthcare in patient safety.

There is very little on offer to help people develop this expertise apart from the odd day at a conference. People struggle on their own to figure out this hugely complex subject. Imagine conducting a full root cause analysis of an incident that had directly led to one or more deaths with no training or experience. Imagine talking to a parent about the serious life-threatening error that their child has been affected by with no training or experience. Imagine trying to get a whole organisation to change a particular procedure or piece of equipment that they are all wedded to doing or using, with no training or experience.

In relation to risk management and incident investigation in the UK, too often these vital roles are now relegated to counting and data collection. Risk management is seen as tedious and bureaucratic. The people responsible for clinical risk are expected to collect incidents, investigate, implement change, share learning, audit and review implementation while at the same time engage and provide information and support to distressed patients, their families and the staff who care for them. They are constrained by timelines and the quest for completing the investigation is the aim, not the learning; the final report is seen as the end product, not the start. Investigators in the National Health Service (NHS) do not have an army of personnel to examine the incident reports they are faced with – they are more likely to be confronted with an army of inspectors instead. The function has shifted from finding out stuff and fixing it to meeting the needs of external inspection and scrutiny. The skills and tools needed are consistently underused and their potential under realised and, dare I say it, with the ever-increasing emphasis on quality improvement, we are in danger of losing our way and relegating these key components of safety to being simple administrative tasks.

This is in a context where people are potentially blinkered by the pursuit of the wrong kind of excellence – usually productive and financial indicators and the imperative need to achieve these targets.

## Incident Investigation

People who have a role in clinical risk and patient safety have learnt to do the job, on the job. Their role is unpredictable and huge. They are often unable to use the work of experts because they are constantly being reactive and tackling one incident at a time, and the dream they have of capturing and learning from near misses is just that – a dream. People don't have the time to do justice to what is needed. They make recommendations that they know are weak suggestions for training and protocols because the stronger ones involve changing whole systems and they don't really have the mandate or the authority to do that. They don't have enough support because those in turn who are expected to support them don't have the time to do so.

In order to address this, organisations should employ individuals who are skilled in systems thinking, human factors, cognitive interviewing, behavioural change, mediation, facilitation and delivering difficult news, and who can also gain the trust of all around them, the patient and their family and the staff involved and help create the right conversations 'from one human being to another'. These organisations will finally be able to start addressing the risks in their organisation, start to reduce the chances of error and reduce avoidable harm and improve patient safety.

It takes enormous skill to conduct an investigation well. Investigators need to help people remember what happened, what they did or what others did. They need to carry out the investigation in an unbiased way; unbiased by the outcome of the incident, by hindsight and their own confirmative bias which skews their ability to see the truth. They need to try to see beyond these, get beneath the surface of what can be seen and learn from the data that are not there and go beyond the lessons that are superficial.

Investigators need to learn and use an accident causality model (Leveson 2012). Models explain why errors and incidents occur and determine the approaches we need to take in order to prevent them from happening again. The underlying assumption of these models is that there are common patterns in incidents and that they are not simply random events (Reason 1990, Leveson 2012). The model most used in healthcare is that of root cause analysis, which also uses the 'swisscheese' model of error (Reason 1990). The problem with these models is that they perpetuate the myth that there is a neat chain of events or failures which directly cause or lead to the next one on the chain.

Incident investigations need to involve a review of the entire system and to make recommendations for that system. Currently, recommendations are often short-term fixes that will not lead to sustained change. Recommendations such as a new protocol, training for staff, reminding staff to be safer or suspending staff do not prevent the incident from ever happening again.

Also, the changes we put in place, however good or bad they are, erode over time – we are very good at focusing intensely on something for a short while but we all take our eyes off the ball and resort to our original habits and behaviours unless we make fundamental design changes to the system that make it hard for people to revert to old habits.

In the UK, a review by the Public Administration Select Commitee (PASC 2015) called for a strengthened investigative capacity in front-line healthcare organisations supported by, where possible, independent expertise to provide national leadership, to serve as a resource of skills and expertise for the conduct of patient safety incident investigations and to act as a catalyst to promote a just and open culture across a whole health system. They called for a new body to oversee the system of incident investigations: the *Healthcare Safety Investigations Branch*. I could only have dreamt of such a thing as a young risk manager.

They listed three areas of good practice that could be used as a framework for all investigations:

■ Find the facts and evidence early, without the need to find blame
■ Strengthen investigative capacity locally and support people
■ Provide leadership and a resource of skills and expertise that also acts as a catalyst to promote a just and open culture

The committee also recommended (PASC 2015):

■ That human factors and incident analysis be part of the training of all healthcare professionals
■ The development of a body of professionally qualified investigative staff with formal examinations and qualifications

If the recommendations made by these various opinions and reports actually happen, we could transform the way we learn and improve patient safety. This is a massive opportunity. To build on this, the view of people who work in risk, patient safety and investigation needs to change; they should not be seen as the enemy.

The quote referred to earlier by Professor Graham Braithwaite of Cranfield University (PASC 2015) – that aviation investigators are regarded in the industry as credible and trustworthy and it is a role that is seen by many as the pinnacle of their career – was so profound for me. For someone who has spent a large part of their career in risk and patient safety, I would be really proud to think that I was at the pinnacle of my career.

## Suggested Reading

*Black Box Thinking* by Matthew Syed, published in 2015 by John Murray Publishers, is a fascinating view of learning from error with examples across healthcare and other high-risk industries as well as lessons from sports science such as the 'marginal gains' concepts used, particularly in elite cycling.

*Close Calls*, written by Carl Macrae and published in 2014, provides valuable knowledge on risk and resilience, incident investigations, analysing risk and creating organisational resilience.

## Chapter 8

# The Impact on Front-Line Workers

I will be more careful in the future.

**Kimberley Hyatt**
*2011*

## Reflective Observation

A few years after my own personal experience of error, I carried out a retrospective investigation in order to finally understand why it happened. I learnt that tiredness, distractions and stress are all contributory factors to error and that there were 'human factors' that meant that my mind could play tricks with me. I learnt that drug errors are particularly prone to this and that paediatric errors are frequent because of the complex calculations that are required for children. Children's medications often have to be calculated because they are specifically dosed according to their weight. Sadly, I learnt that 'ten times the dose' is a 'classic' medication error and is something that has been happening to children in particular for decades.

I now know that, rather than being solely down to individuals, there were a number of small moments or incidents
during my shift that led me to miscalculate the drug – the
constant distractions, automaticity, human factors and being
interrupted mid-task, combined with my sleep deprivation
and together with human error, all contributed to the young
boy receiving ten times the dose of a drug. My response
was that I would try harder, that I would not make any
more errors, but this perpetuates the myth of perfection.
We all need to accept the fact that people, processes and
equipment will fail. By understanding this, organisations
can focus on developing defences and contingency plans to
cope with these failures. If instead we simply punish people
when they make errors, we will not learn about the underlying conditions that may have caused the error. When staff
are fearful of repercussions and blame, it hinders them from
sharing their concerns and speaking up when things go
wrong. This, in turn, means that mistakes can be hidden,
issues can be buried and lessons go unlearned (Berwick
2013).

Not only did James Reason help me understand the
nuances of human error, he also helped me come to terms
with my own experience of harm and the importance of sup-
porting people involved in error and harm so that they can
cope with their experience. I knew that, not only the two
nurses caught up in the incident, but the entire unit should
have been supported.

What we needed was to all talk to each other about what
happened; talk to each other about what we all thought could
be done differently. What we also needed to do was learn to
talk to the families of the children we cared for. To have conversations that help people feel confident to speak out when
things go wrong. If we had had these conversations, people
would have learnt more about what they can do to make their
care safer and if we had known all of that, who knows how
many children could have been saved from harm?

# Bob's Story

In 2016, I came across a radio interview with Bob Ebeling. Bob was one of the engineers working on the shuttle Challenger 30 years ago; since the radio interview, Bob has died. This was his story (Berkes 2016). On 27 January 1986, Bob, the engineer, had joined four of his colleagues in trying to keep the space shuttle Challenger grounded. They argued for hours that the launch the next morning would be the coldest ever. Freezing temperatures (their data showed) stiffened the rubber O-rings that keep burning rocket fuel from leaking out of the joints in the shuttle's boosters. For more than 30 years, Bob has carried the guilt of the Challenger explosion. He was an engineer and he knew the shuttle couldn't sustain the freezing temperatures. He warned his supervisors. He told his wife it was going to blow up. The next morning it did, just as he said it would, and seven astronauts died. Bob was simply not listened to.

Since that tragic day, Bob blamed himself. He always wondered whether he could have done more. That day changed him. He became steeped in his own grief, despondent and withdrawn. He quit his job. Bob, at 89, spoke on National Public Radio (NPR), a radio station in the United States, on the 30th anniversary of the Challenger explosion. If you listen to the recording, you can hear his voice; it is low, quiet and heavy with sadness as he recalled the day and described his three decades of guilt. 'I think that was one of the mistakes that God made', he said. 'He [God] shouldn't have picked me for the job. But next time I talk to him, I'm gonna ask him …"Why me? You picked a loser"'.

The listeners were so moved by this that they sent hundreds of e-mails and letters of support to Bob. Engineering teachers said they would use him as an example of good ethical practice and other professionals wrote that, because of his example, they are more vigilant in their jobs. Allan McDonald, who was Bob's boss at the time, contacted him and told him that he had done everything he could have done to warn them: 'The decision was a collective decision made by all of us. You should not torture yourself with any assumed blame'. And NASA issued a statement commending courageous people like Bob, who they said 'speak up so that our astronauts can safely carry out their missions'.

While this story relates to space travel, there are strong synergies with the way healthcare practitioners have, across the centuries, tried to speak out and were not listened to. If Bob had been listened to, he may have been able to prevent the death of seven astronauts. There are similarities also with the way those affected by error live with the guilt and share it for the rest of their lives, profoundly and forever affected by these events. We need to care for them, be kind to them, support them to come to terms with what went on and never be judgmental. Speaking from my own experience, the guilt never goes away but a kind word goes a very long way to help. Every healthcare facility should provide an after-event duty of care to all, a function that supports patients, their relatives and staff when things go wrong.

There is an exceptionally moving piece at the very end of the *British Medical Journal* (*BMJ*) in March 2000 (Anon – Looking back ... 2000). It was a personal account of the death of a patient, which the writer says was 'at my hands'. He tells us about how he sat down with the family and explained what went wrong and why and how he listened to the anger directed at him. He says it was the hardest thing he had ever done. His way of coming through this was by talking to his family and to a 'valued friend' who went through the whole event step by step to slowly make some sense of the events. He also talks about times when talking to others was 'clumsy'; while someone in the middle of a crowded room at a conference asked him how he was, others just ignored him. He said it was 6 months before his heart stopped leaping at the letters marked private and confidential. He thought his life was back to normal until his partner asked a very simple question, why his behaviour was erratic. He tells us that, within minutes, he was in tears and hopelessly out of control, and it was only then he realised that it was not about getting over it but more about trying to live with it.

Albert Wu made the case, as far back as the year 2000, for helping others feel safe to talk about mistakes by encouraging them to describe what happened and to talk about the emotional impact. He talked about the importance of asking colleagues how they are and how they are coping. He talked about how important, while extremely difficult, it is to talk to the patient and/or their family and how that conversation can in itself be healing. Wu also talked of the wider team who may bear 'silent witness' to mistakes, agonise over conflicting loyalties and not know who to talk to about what they know. Only once these conversations have been held should the team start to explore the event with a problem-solving focus on what could be done differently and what changes are needed. He concluded his article with a simple assignment: think back to your last mistake that harmed a patient and go and talk to a colleague about it. Notice the colleague's reaction and your own.

## Kimberley's Story

We have seen how people can experience guilt, anxiety, depression and more. They find themselves reliving the event days, weeks, months and sometimes years later. They are often devastated and it can lead to their lives unravelling. Anecdotal evidence suggests that unsupported health workers may also change their place of work or leave, and some even leave the career altogether. Well-trained, caring, experienced nurses and doctors are moving on, either to another hospital or another career altogether.

Albert Wu (2000), who is renowned for his work in helping clinicians come to terms with their mistakes, talks about the 'second victim', clinicians who have been involved in an error or patient injury, and their attendant sense of guilt and remorse. He eloquently describes what it feels like when, as a clinician, you make a bad mistake; the feeling of being singled out, exposed, the questioning of competence, the fear and the lack of 'unconditional sympathy and support' (Wu 2000).

If people could talk to each other about these experiences, Wu felt that it would allow others to come forward to share with the rest of the group. Active communication should be encouraged but we lack the appropriate forums for this kind of discussion and there are no institutional mechanisms for helping the grieving process that all clinicians go through. Even if mistakes are talked about at morbidity and mortality meetings, it is usually just to examine the facts and not the feelings of the people involved. In the absence of the mechanisms to help people talk to each other, people respond with anger and blame or they may turn to substance abuse, give up their careers or even their lives.

Every now and then, I google 'ten times the dose' and, without fail, there will be references and links to medication errors almost exactly like the one I was involved in. During one of these searches, I came across a story from 2011 that took my breath away (Kliff 2016). The story was about Kimberley Hiatt, a paediatric intensive care nurse in the United States.

Kimberley was, just like me, a nurse who worked in PICU, although her story took place 20 years later. As the result of a 'ten times the dose incident', one of the children in her care died. A doctor instructed Kimberley to administer 140 mg of calcium chloride to her patient, a 9-month-old infant. She worked out the dosage in her head because she had administered calcium chloride hundreds of times. She, in error, miscalculated and drew up ten times the dose prescribed.

Similar to the incident I was involved in, a doctor noticed something was wrong. He noticed that the child's heart rate was increasing and a blood test showed a rise in the calcium levels. When she explained to another nurse what she had done, they both realised the error. I read about Kimberley's interview for the investigation. She said she had messed up, that she was talking to someone while drawing it up and she told them that she would be more careful in the future. Almost immediately after the interview, Kimberley was escorted off the premises. I cannot imagine how that must have felt. Kimberley was not a bad person. She loved her job, she loved her patients. All of a sudden, she was isolated from the job, her colleagues and the hospital where she had worked for over 24 years. We are told that she drove home panicking about what had happened.

You can see that she felt she was personally and solely culpable for this incident. She also gave us clues as to why the incident happened: distraction, automaticity, calculating in her head. 'I will be more careful in the future' is not a recommendation for sustained change. Four days later, the child died, and shortly after that Kimberley was fired. She struggled with the death of the patient and the loss of the career she loved. Sadly, she never got over this incident and 7 months after she was walked off the premises she committed suicide.

The changes made in the hospital rightly focused on preventing the incident from happening again. However, if the solution was to remove the nurse from the situation, it's the wrong one – that does not lead to sustained change.

There is one key lesson from this story – the hospital did not learn from the other tragedy that took place, the nurse's anxiety and subsequent suicide. In fact, in Kimberley's case, one of the employees said they felt that people were still afraid to admit their mistakes, based on what had happened to Kimberley. They suggested that people didn't admit mistakes because they were afraid of losing their jobs (Kliff 2016). It is vital to the memory of healthcare workers like Kimberley that healthcare providers take healthcare workers' grief seriously.

## Richie's Story

In writing his *A Life in Error*, Jim Reason (2015) says that he has discovered two key principles: learn as much as possible about the details of how people work and, most importantly, never be judgmental. I learnt these things one July morning in 1997. While at Great Ormond Street Hospital, a group of us were involved in investigating the heartbreaking death of one of the children in our care.

One of the patients, a 12-year-old boy called Richie William, had been wrongly injected into his spine with a chemotherapy drug called vincristine. My heart flipped at the sound of the urgency and fear in the voice that told me this. I wasn't even sure if there was a problem – at that point, I had never even heard of vincristine, let alone the impact. Five minutes later, I am sitting in a room full of oncologists explaining to me that giving vincristine into the spine was usually fatal. They tried to explain the whole process of chemotherapy cycles using complex scientific language that they understood completely whereas I only understood every tenth word. This is one of the problems with healthcare investigations – normal practice can be understood by just a few, while different people and different specialties can have a language all of their own. So we did just as Jim said – we learnt as much as possible.

It soon became clear that the anaesthetist who had administered the drug knew nothing about the fact that Richie had been readmitted with these worrying signs. Even now, I can feel the dread when we walked over to find him. I wanted to be anywhere else but there. I knew fundamentally that this was not the time to be judgmental; this was the time to be kind, to use every skill I had learnt as a nurse in breaking bad news. I shall never forget his face when it dawned on him what had happened.

This young junior doctor's life and that of many others in the hospital were never going to be the same again. Richie's life was taken away from him; he was irreplaceable and his mum and family were devastated. 'You have killed my child', she screamed desperately. So to do justice for Richie and for everyone involved, we vowed to find out as much as possible about what had gone wrong and to learn the lessons for the future.

A small group of us were tasked with investigating Richie's death as part of an internal inquiry, which was chaired by the director of nursing at the hospital. The terms of reference for the inquiry, and therefore the investigation, were to find out what had happened throughout Richie's admission, looking far beyond the final moments. We were tasked with talking to every member of staff, right across the hospital: the pharmacist who made up the chemotherapy, the bed managers who moved Richie from one ward to another, the oncologists, anaesthetists, operating department staff, nurses, managers, senior nurses, consultants and finally Richie's mum.

The chemotherapy was reconstructed, the theatre recreated and interview after interview was held. Slowly we pieced the story together until we felt we had as true a reflection of what had happened as we could. Too often, investigations try to create a simple linear story rather than the complex reality of multiple and interacting factors and events. We found out so much detail that I could even picture Richie's day.

Richie arrived early for his chemotherapy from home. There wasn't room on his normal ward that day so he was admitted onto a different ward that didn't specialise in oncology or chemotherapy. The relocation of patients was normal at the time. He was playing with his handheld games console when he was visited by the anaesthetist. Because Richie was fearful of the procedure that was needed for his chemotherapy, a needle into his spine, his previous doses had been given while he was under a general anaesthetic. The anaesthetist checked with Richie and his mum about how long he had been fasting for. It was then that Richie confessed that he had been really hungry when he woke up and had eaten some biscuits. As a result, the anaesthetist suggested to them both that perhaps this time the procedure could be done without a general anaesthetic. They both agreed. Because of this, Richie was moved from the anaesthetic list and the ward nurses were told that he would be called to come to theatre for the administration just prior to the afternoon lists. So, in effect, he was being squeezed in between the morning and afternoon sessions.

Richie's chemotherapy – two drugs, one for his spine and one for his veins – arrived onto the ward from the specialist pharmacy unit so that the nurse could take it down to theatre with Richie. In the meantime, the anaesthetist wanted to check that he knew what he was doing so he rang the haematologist and asked simply 'do I just inject the drugs?' to which the reply was a simple, 'yes'.

Richie was taken down to theatre at around midday and greeted by the same anaesthetist he had met in the morning. Richie was placed on the theatre couch, nervously holding the hand of the nurse who had walked down with him. All the equipment, together with the chemotherapy syringes, was placed on a sterile field on top of a theatre trolley for the anaesthetist to easily pick up. We were told that there was no conversation between the anaesthetist and his assistant about which drug was which, and that it was a given that these were the right drugs and all the anaesthetist had to do was to look at the labelling of the syringes.

What followed was uneventful, or so they thought. An intrathecal needle was placed in his spine, a cannula placed in a vein. The two drugs were administered and checked between the anaesthetist and the operating department practitioner. Richie went back up to the ward. At this point, no one knew that the two drugs had been mixed up and that both had been given by the wrong route.

Richie went home that evening – it was a Friday. By Sunday, he was feeling extremely unwell. The vincristine that had been injected wrongly into his spine was taking effect. He was admitted back to the hospital, this time onto the specialist haematology unit. It was from there that I was rung that Monday morning. I quickly found out in that first week that vincristine, if injected into the spine, is usually either fatal or leads to paralysis. The patient's only chance of survival is if the error is realised quickly and a washout of the drug is performed. Unbeknown to me, there had been a bit of history related to the inappropriate administration of vincristine. In 1968, 48 years ago, vincristine was first administered intrathecally in error to a young patient with acute lymphocytic leukaemia. She died 3 days later.

Richie died 5 days after admission. Richie was a young, 12–year-old boy who died in our care – as human beings, we are intrinsically motivated to find someone to blame. We are also likely to immediately judge the actions on that day as careless or incompetent. We knew that there would be people who would find it hard to comprehend a decision not to blame or punish the people involved. We knew that we ourselves would judge the past events as somehow more foreseeable than they were, or that what we now knew would colour our perceptions of how and why things occurred. These were not bad people, so we purposefully put these things to one side and looked through the holes in the system.

The result of our collective efforts was a report that we submitted to Richie's mum, the police and the Department of Health in the UK. It was never simply about one person's actions. What we found was an insight into the very workings of a busy and complex children's hospital. We learnt that healthcare is never neat or linear; it is possible to do tasks and activities in healthcare in multiple different orders and multiple ways. What we found was that, as Carl Macrae says, by *noticing, understanding and learning about the small moments* in Richie's life that day, we could piece together the reasons why he was eventually injected with the wrong drug into the wrong route.

The report could have been summed up in one paragraph – Richie died because of a combination of small changes to everyday events, last minute deviations from the normal routine, distractions, unclear communication, plus the poor design of packaging, mixed together with human error. The final report, we were told eventually, helped clear the two doctors of a manslaughter charge. In the words of the judge, the internal investigation described a chapter of accidents and misunderstandings, a catalogue of chance events and failings at the hospital rather than gross negligence by the doctors.

During the investigation into the death of Richie William, we also found out that the exact same incident had happened across the globe and, by then, at least 12 times in British hospitals. Clearly, learning from one incident to another was virtually non-existent. This is an example of exactly what Sir Liam Donaldson meant when he wanted to create a national reporting and learning system. His vision was one of staff identifying a problem one day and sharing that right across the NHS the next, to enable system-wide learning. Instead, we have incident reporting systems that are drowning. What we didn't know at the time of our investigation was that there would be another incident 3 years later at Queens Medical Centre in Nottingham, the now well-known case of Wayne Jowett. Was there anything that we could have done that would have prevented Wayne from dying too?

There is one key lesson from this story – at the heart of this tragic case was a simple set of poor conversations, the confused conversation between the anaesthetist and the haematologist and the lack of conversation between the anaesthetist and his operating department practitioner. If these people had talked to each other more effectively, it may have prevented the wrong drug from being administered via the wrong route.

We need to help all of those people like Bob Ebeling, Kimberley Hyatt or the anonymous storyteller. The people like them who are living with the guilt and shame and the people who are profoundly and forever affected by these events. It is our belief that they need to be cared for, that they need kindness and not punishment and are supported to come to terms with what went on.

## Suggested Reading

*A Life in Error*, written by James Reason and published in 2013, is a personal and intimate trip through human error, risk management and safety that is written in his own unique style.

*Chapter 9*

# The Implementation Challenge

The approach of relying on passive diffusion of information to inform health professionals about safer practices, is doomed to failure in a global environment in which well over two million articles on clinical issues are published annually.

**Suzette Woodward**
*2008*

## Just Do It

It is easy to have an idea or design a device or write a guideline that should work if implemented. The hard part is to take the idea, device or guidance and make it work well every time. Yet, who has not attended a conference focused on quality or safety and not been frustrated with the comments 'Let's create a new policy', or 'create a checklist', or 'why is it so hard for people to simply do the right thing?' This over-simplistic model of implementation is characterised by 'why don't they just do it'. This model assumes that, once the idea or solution has been designed, the staff will simply carry out the actions required.

Implementation is a complex process, not a one-off event. It is the multiple steps required to take a piece of research, good idea or good practice and turn it into action. If the good idea is picked up or adopted by individuals and then used on a day-to-day basis, it is then said to be embedded. If the good idea is then shared across to other individuals, it is described as spread. If the good idea sticks and people continue to be different as a result, it is said to be sustained. Implementation, therefore, is the combined process of dissemination, adoption, embedding, spread and sustainability of good ideas.

However, at every stage of that process, people can and do get it wrong. It is not nearly as simple as people think. In healthcare, the traditional approach to implementation is to do the first step – simply disseminate the good idea and expect the 'audience' to pick it up and run with it. The approach with guidance or alerts is mainly one of distribution to a passive group of people who may not even notice that it has arrived.

In patient safety, there are lots of good ideas about keeping patients safer or reducing harm. There are the large top-down interventions, but implementation is not always about making a large change; in fact, it is often about making small incremental changes that can make things easier, better, more effective and safer. It is, in fact, sometimes easier to make changes because of a defining moment. Making changes after a major incident or catastrophe has a stronger chance of success because of the motivation caused by the incident itself. One of the key questions here is, are those changes embedded and sustained?

The harder thing to do is to convince people to change on a daily basis, to consider every small decision made and ask whether that decision could have been a better one. It is also harder to convince people to change if they don't see a significant and large effect. Visible outcomes are always great motivators, whether you want to lose weight or reduce the number of falls or pressure ulcers. Seeing the graph go down or the weight go off are great ways in which to convince people to continue. What if you can't see them? Most change is not an earth-shattering improvement that everyone will want to talk about and share. However, improving in a small way can be just as meaningful. The difficulty here is noticing whether there is a difference over time and being able to recognise it enough to continue to do the same thing. Even those who are making the decisions may not be aware of the impact that they are making. It would help to get beneath the surface of what is going on every day to try to understand these choices and notice if they lead to a small improvement or even a small decline.

In healthcare, we are drowning in ways in which we could improve – numerous interventions and solutions, lots of research and guidance. National bodies in the UK in particular love to create standards, alerts and 'must-do' notices and targets. For example, there have been repeated alerts published and disseminated in relation to the same topics in healthcare. This should tell us that the method of 'telling people just to do it' isn't working. For example, in the UK, there have been multiple alerts issued over the last 15 years to try to prevent patients from dying as a result of the insertion of a nasogastric tube into the lungs instead of the stomach. The people on the receiving end are expected to implement these changes quickly, often with very little resources to help. What implementation scientists tell us is that guidelines, standards or alerts issued in isolation rarely change people's individual practices (Haines and Donald 1998, Hunter 2002, Woodward 2008). They are, at best, complied with, but they have not been found to drive sustained improvement. This is the gap between what we assume improves patient safety and what is actually done in practice.

## Seven Steps

In the early days of patient safety, many of us fell into the trap of disseminating guidance and expecting change to simply happen as a result, but after a while, we have been forced to admit that things didn't turn out as we had originally intended and planned. In 2003, when I joined the National Patient Safety Agency (NPSA), a group of us pulled together the latest thinking on patient safety and wrote national patient safety guidance for the NHS, titled *Seven Steps to Patient Safety* (Seven Steps) (NPSA 2004, 2005). A significant effort went into producing the guidance, which was based on a combination of a systematic review of the research, assimilation of the international and national patient safety knowledge and understanding, together with personal experience and expertise. We consulted people on the front line and we sought help in writing the guidance so that it was easy to understand and interpret.

Seven Steps was launched at the NPSA's annual conference in 2004 and a copy disseminated to every healthcare facility throughout the National Health Service (NHS) by NPSA staff. The seven steps, which were at the heart of the guidance, were also used as the basis for training over 8000 NHS staff in patient safety. However, despite this seemingly successful dissemination, effective implementation of the suggested strategies did not occur (National Audit Office 2005, Department of Health 2006). Over the following years, we also noticed that compliance with other national interventions and patient safety alerts was not as we had hoped. We started to realise that simply telling people to get on with it was not the answer.

Our ultimate aim was that the guidance would be fully implemented, that is, embedded into everyday practice. We did a number of things wrong. We framed it as guidance and then expected people to adopt it as if it was mandatory and not optional. We failed to provide clear, actionable recommendations; rather, we thought that our audience would completely understand what was meant by 'build a safety culture'. What we also failed to realise was that the approach of relying on passive diffusion of information to inform health professionals about safer practices is doomed to failure in a global environment in which well over two million articles on clinical issues are published annually (Woodward 2008).

Learning about new ideas is a complex issue in healthcare. Clinicians, in the main, are interested in their specialty; they want to get better at exactly what they do. If that is general practice or orthopaedic surgery, then that is the kind of information they want to read about in order to improve. General topics like leadership, quality and patient safety are put in the 'nice to do when I have time' pile. In the main, all of us use knowledge gained through years of training and experience. Occasionally, we may then look outwards at new approaches, innovations and best practice. But in today's context of a mass of instant information, this is a daunting task.

## Vincristine Error

The patients who die in our care deserve nothing more than our commitment to implementing solutions that have been proven to improve safety so that others do not suffer the same fate. That should be the case for Richie William. As you have read, Richie died as a result of being inadvertently administered vincristine into his spine – a 'vincristine error' as it is now referred to. However, Richie's vincristine error was not an isolated event. These errors have happened before and, despite the significant amount of guidance, best practice and alerts, errors have since continued to occur across the world on a regular basis. History is repeating itself time and time again. As we have found, research tells us that embedding new ideas into everyday practice takes on average 17 years; since Richie died, we are at year 19 and counting.

If we study vincristine errors, they provide us with a window into the complexity and difficulties faced in relation to implementation. The following detail is mainly taken from an excellent summary of 'The quest to eliminate intrathecal vincristine errors: A 40 year journey' by Noble and Donaldson (2010). In 2004, in the UK, a review was conducted to assess the level of implementation of guidance for the safe administration of vincristine. This was 3 years after the revised guidance had been issued and disseminated. Despite two very high profile deaths related to vincristine error in the UK, the review revealed only 50% compliance. Despite these tragic events, sustained change had not occurred across the system.

The specific risks of inadvertent administration of vincristine were clearly recognised from the early experience in the 1960s. However, to date, nearly 60 reported cases of intrathecal vincristine errors are known to have occurred, with several others assumed as unreported (Noble and Donaldson 2010). The second reported case was in 1978, a 5-year-old boy with acute lymphocytic leukaemia in the United States, who, like Richie, also received intravenous and intrathecal chemotherapy at the same time. A third death was reported 2 years later, in 1980. This followed a series of publications in specialist journals related to pharmacy practice, paediatrics and cancer treatment. One publication described the treatment of inadvertent intrathecal injection of vincristine in the *New England Journal of Medicine*, focusing on the treatment of the consequences and not the causes of the error (Dyke 1989).

In 1998, following another fatal administration, a medication safety alert was issued by the Institute for Safe Medication Practices in the United States. More incidents followed, so another alert was issued in 2000. Since then, further deaths have been reported in the United States and in Hong Kong. This tells us about the effectiveness of patient safety alerts. If nothing else, those that create these alerts need to understand how lessons from implementation science and behavioural insights could help them change their methods in order to realise their ambitions and prevent vincristine errors.

Since 2001, in the UK, policies have been put in place to reduce the chances of a vincristine error happening by ensuring that the two drugs are never given by the same person, in the same place or even on the same day. The policy for addressing vincristine error includes that

- Cytotoxic drugs should be given only by specialist, appropriately trained staff.
- The dose of vincristine should be diluted to at least 10 ml to help distinguish it from drugs intended for intrathecal injection, for which such a large volume is rarely given.
- All administration devices containing vincristine must be labelled '*Warning: Vincristine: For intravenous use only*', because if it is labelled 'not for' then it is easy for someone to occlude the 'not' so that the administrators only see the word 'for'.
- Intrathecal drugs should be administered in a designated area – for example, an operating theatre.
- Drugs for intrathecal use should be delivered to the point of use from the pharmacy at a different time to and packed separately from all other drugs.
- No other cytotoxic drugs should be delivered to, stored in or administered in the designated area.

The gold standard for reducing or even eliminating risk is to design out the ability for the risk to be realised, to prevent the risk leading to error or harm (Norman 2013). In relation to vincristine errors, the design solution is to change the connections of both the intrathecal syringe and the intravenous cannula to make it impossible to attach an intravenous syringe to a spinal needle. One should never be able to fit the other. This is described as a forcing function, making it virtually physically impossible to take the wrong action.

Implementation of the design change has been an enormous uphill task and we are still not quite there yet in terms of total compliance (Noble and Donaldson 2010). For example, a spinal injection safety system developed in Canada has shown some promise but has not yet been used widely (Sheppard et al. 2006). The Department of Health in the UK has been pursuing a plan to implement a system to eliminate all 'Luer' connections associated with spinal delivery systems, but apparently progress is slow due to the complexities of designing an entirely new connection system. Manufacturers, we are told, have also been reluctant to invest in development when they believe there is little demand and no major market for a new product. However, in Japan, following the death of a patient, there has been some success when a significant change was made to connectors on syringes in just under a year following the incident (Bickford Smith 2001).

Rather than wait for the design solution, alternative solutions have been sought. In recent years, the use of a minibag to deliver vincristine has become increasingly discussed and advocated. This is not a full physical design solution or forcing function, but offers an interim measure. It involves not using syringes to deliver vincristine at all and instead diluting the drug in a minibag, working on the premise that it would be virtually impossible to deliver this to a patient through a spinal needle. An alert issued by the National Patient Safety Agency (NPSA) in 2008 stated that no incidents had been reported where a minibag had been used (NPSA 2008). The World Health Organization (WHO) published an alert immediately following the death of a patient in Hong Kong in July 2007, and recommended using the minibag to prevent errors in the absence of a more formal design solution (WHO 2007).

In China, in 2007, two drugs normally given intrathecally (methotrexate and cytarabine hydrochloride) were contaminated with vincristine at the factory level (Noble and Donaldson 2010). At first, a few children in Shanghai and Guangxi Zhuang Autonomous Region suffered neurological symptoms. Paralysis was common, and these incidents increased the world total for vincristine errors from 58 to 251 overnight. Eventually, the outbreak was believed to have led to 193 patients across China having received intrathecal vincristine unintentionally. The Chinese government recalled the drugs and closed the plant. As Noble and Donaldson report, unusual events like this do not get reported via incident reporting systems and even the best design solution may not have prevented such an unpredictable and 'upstream' form of error. Yet, this story keeps us attentive to the ongoing dangers in every aspect of healthcare, from factory to front line, and adds another vulnerability to this long-running story of unsafe care.

## To Checklist or Not to Checklist

Change, as we have seen, mainly happens when a sum of actions is combined. In isolation, each action would not make a major difference, but joined together they make a powerful difference. This is the story of the WHO Surgical Checklist. The checklist was designed in 2006–2007 and tested in the UK in 2008 with an implementation roll out in 2009. With regard to the checklist content, individual teams were allowed to adapt it to fit with their environment while keeping the core of the checklist the same. Roll out included the use of opinion leaders, local surgical champions who would visibly support the use of the checklist.

I had the honour of being one of a handful of people representing England at the meetings of the over 50 member states of the WHO in relation to the development of a global checklist to enhance surgical safety. This challenge was being led by Atul Gawande, whose fame preceded him. In 2002, Atul Gawande had written a book called *Complications* (Gawande 2002). To this date, this remains one of the most interesting, engaging and insightful books on patient safety that exists. One of the unique aspects of the book is that Gawande used storytelling to turn a potentially dry subject into a fascinating page turner. A later book, *The Checklist Manifesto: How to Get Things Right* (Gawande 2009) beautifully described the challenges people face in implementing checklists from a number of stories across the world and ultimately makes the case for why using a checklist is worth it.

It remains astonishing to me today that the final checklist designed had the approval of over 50 different countries from across the globe. To all come together and agree on the core components of what should and should not be included in a simple one-page checklist is astounding. It is important to remember this achievement in the light of the criticisms that have followed since.

The checklist was, on the face of it, a list of things to check off prior to surgery. However, it was clearly more than a list. To work, it needed to be supported by the use of briefing and debriefing. It also required significant changes to teamwork, culture and workflow. Properly used, the checklist ensures that critical tasks are carried out and that the whole team is adequately prepared for the surgical operation. For example, the checklist briefing allows each member of the team to introduce themselves and review information given by the others, embedding the importance of clear and consistent communication from the beginning of the theatre session and before every single operation. The checklist builds on the same principles found in aviation, which is to ensure that individuals, whether they have worked together before or not, feel an equal part of the team and have the ability to speak out if they have any concerns, either before, during or after the operation. During the implementation process, in the main, anaesthetists and nurses were largely supportive of the checklist but consultant surgeons were not convinced.

There has been some debate about the impact of the surgical checklist on reducing avoidable harm or saving lives. Checklists in themselves do not prevent or reduce harm; it is the way in which the checklists are used that can do this. At its simplest, the desire by Gawande was to enable team members to stop and take a moment simply to talk with one another before proceeding. Critically, checklists are not enough on their own to create good working relationships. Correct use of the checklist has been found to lead to a reduction in mortality (from 1.5% to 0.8%) and morbidity (11% to 7%) (Haynes et al. 2009).

There is clearly a difference between implementation and compliance. Initially, data suggested that, in the UK, we achieved almost complete adoption in the first year. However, what we now know is that there is huge variability in use and implementation. People think that if you implement the main bits, you will still receive the total benefit. The checklist, to work, requires all of the component parts to be implemented, but in the main, around half of it is used. In some organisations, we found that components of the checklist were missed out or incomplete. `for example, the sign-out and debrief post checklist were particularly poorly carried out. The risk with this is that if you only implement some of the checklist then you may end up receiving none of the benefits. It is a bit like having a car with everything except the wheels; while the wheels are a small percentage of the car, you can't drive it without them (Lindland et al. 2015).

Additionally, people didn't expect implementation to require ongoing maintenance. There are examples of what appears to be robust implementation and 100% compliance, but then people become complacent and compliance drops. Poor practice starts to erode good practice; in some organisations, the checklists are completed prior to the theatre session or prior to the patient even arriving into the anaesthetic room. In some, we will find that there is pressure on individual people to comply with the checklist quickly, as if it is something that just has to be done rather than a valuable tool for the team to come together and ensure that the rest of the day runs smoothly. In part, people find checklists useful in the beginning but, when it starts to become routine, the checklist becomes boring. People start to not bother, thinking that as they have carried it out time and time again they know what is needed so they leave the checklist aside. For implementation to 'stick', it should be adapted to local context and then continuously maintained.

In aviation, the mentality is completely different. Checklists are used constantly, and even if the individuals in the cockpit have used the same checklist for pre-flight checking for years and years, they will take the time and effort to do it every single time. This is the same for engineers who, when stripping an aircraft for routine maintenance, use the checklist every single time even though their experience and expertise is telling them they know what they are doing and what they are looking for. This is because pilots and engineers have been taught that human beings are fallible, that they are easily distracted and can easily forget a step or two. Using checklists for these people is a way of life and not simply a task.

## Suggested Reading

*The Checklist Manifesto*. Published by Profile Books in 2010 and written by Atul Gawande, this is a masterpiece describing the story of checklists. If you are in any doubt as to whether checklists can improve patient safety, all you need to do is read this book and you will be convinced.

## Chapter 10

# Implementation: The Way Forward

It takes, on average, 17 years to turn 14% of original research findings into practice.

**Suzette Woodward**
*2008*

## What Can We Do Differently for Implementation?

The recognition of the failure of our approach at the National Patient Safety Agency (NPSA) led to my pursuing a doctorate in patient safety implementation and to greater awareness of the role of the factors that can help and hinder effective implementation (Woodward 2008). What did I find out? There is not enough written on how to execute or how to implement, and there is not enough research around how implementation occurs and under what conditions it's favourable. However, there is a growing science of implementation. This is the study of methods to promote the systematic uptake of research findings and other evidence-based practices into routine practice (Eccles and Mittman 2006). The field of implementation, like patient safety, is a relatively young one. There are other parallels with patient safety. As with any emerging field, there are differing opinions on terminology, concepts, theories and effective interventions.

Implementation science draws mainly from the disciplines of evidence-based medicine and guidance implementation together with the diffusion of innovation, change management, organisational development and behavioural change theories. This field has now an evidence base that informs people about the core components of implementation and implementation practice (Eccles and Mittman 2006, Woodward 2008). It is about studying each aspect of implementation plus the reasons for the gap between ideas and practice and understanding how to narrow or bridge this gap (Woodward 2008).

Implementation requires thoughtful action; it requires expertise and effort, and there is no easy way of doing it. I learned that each stage, dissemination, adoption, embedding, spread and sustainability requires special thought. I learned all about the many factors or principles that can be used in order to maximise the chances of the good idea being finally sustained. Very few get it right; effective implementation of knowledge, research and information in healthcare practice remains, for many, an unconquered challenge. Implementation is a slow and haphazard process (Eccles and Mittman 2006, Woodward 2008). To my surprise, implementation research has found that it takes, on average, 17 years to turn 14% of original research findings into practice (Woodward 2008). If we look at the question I asked earlier, when we actually do change or implement a change, is it sustained in the long term? What I learnt was that even when implemented in some way, we fall at the final hurdle; there is a sustainability failure rate of up to 70% for organisational change (Elwyn et al. 2007).

Implementation requires dedicated resources, funding and time and a shift away from the short-term approach to change and implementation. It is a fantasy to think that an idea can be implemented through to sustained change in just 3 to 5 years. This is, in part, because implementation requires a culture shift; a culture whereby the embedded idea is still used, even when politics, policies or people change. Understanding the simple reality that implementation takes times is important, but we can also aim to reduce the time from the average of 17 years.

We can study implementation science to support patient safety science and focus on the delivery of safety policy, recommendations, research and theory so that it is adopted, spread and embedded into everyday practice. As I have said, there is an overwhelming amount of new knowledge or new initiatives generated each year by clinical research, standard setters and policy makers. But every day, the 'every day' gets in the way of noticing anything new. How do we help people to notice the things they need when they may only have 5 minutes in their day to sit down and look beyond their daily activity?

Implementation can never be a passive process. To choose to move to a new practice means that people have to give up on the old practice. However, if the perception is that the old practice is just fine, then what is the incentive? A primary aim should be to demonstrate that there is an explicit need for the change or the solution and that the proposed solution is the right one for the context and problem.

## Factors That Hinder and Help

There are a number of influencing factors that can both help and hinder effective implementation. The best approaches are when individual methods to support implementation are used in combination with each other. For example, an alert in isolation or training in isolation will not lead to successful implementation, but combining an alert with training may make a difference.

The list of factors that affect the success of adoption and implementation includes the following (Jones et al. 2016, Woodward 2008, Shojania and Catchpole 2015):

- Demonstrate visibly with numbers, feelings and experiences that the change is better than the status quo.
- Deliver the message in person; use the person, the right role model or opinion leader to convince others of the need to change; people will implement changes that are liked by other people who do a similar job, and those people are respected.
- Make it as easy and as intuitive as possible; pick up a well-known 'tablet' and before you know it you have accessed the Internet, sent some e-mails and followed a few people on Twitter – the product is that simple.
- Factor in the fact that people don't have the time.
- Improve the quality of the guidance associated with the idea or solution; do not produce a 100-page manual.
- Reduce reliance on hours of training.
- Understand the receptive context; appreciate the complexity of a problem or the context in which it is required.
- Test it, adapt it, test it, adapt it and test it again to get everyone to feel it fits for them – shift from the notion that something that works in another country, another organisation or even another team will automatically work for you.
- Use a variety of intrinsic and extrinsic incentives; the incentive needs to match the norms, values and working methods of the individuals, teams or organisation implementing it. Different people have different intrinsic motivators, learning styles and approaches to change – some are innovators or early adopters, others are competitive; most prefer positive feedback.
- Reward and recognise people for their actions, and thank and value them for their contribution to safer care.

- Invest resources dedicated to implementation, including protected time for staff.
- Target the right audience and help them to own the change and choose things that they want to change because it improves their everyday activity.
- Leaders need to use a coaching style of leadership; if they simply try to solve the problems themselves, then people will not own the outcome.
- The right choice of method of implementation is vital (Greenhalgh et al. 2005).

Test whether the design or idea remains the right tool, which remains so even after continuous use. For example, in general practice in the UK, doctors have computerised prescribing systems. When the GP (general practitioner) prescribes a new drug for a patient, the system will alert the GP if the proposed drug will interact with one of their other drugs or the dose appears too high. This is an attempt to stop the GP from prescribing a particular drug to a patient. This sounds like a good thing but because the alerts appear relatively often, they can become irritating, and so instead of paying attention to the alerts, the GP simply 'clicks them off' when they appear. This happens in a similar way with alarms associated with heart monitors or infusion pumps.

The world we live and work in is complex so the notion of a single approach or that, once implemented, the job is done must be rejected. Consequently, the problem of implementation needs to be owned by all of us – those who develop the guidance, alert or intervention and those who are on the receiving end. Whether you are a researcher, developer or policy maker, you have to design your 'change' with an implementation strategy from the beginning. All of us need to better understand behavioural change theories, including motivation and social learning theory, together with lessons from the behavioural insights world, why some people change and why others wait a while (Rogers 1983, 1995).

- Design: Make sure that guidance and standards are in date and talk to people who know the situation better than anyone else at the design stage.
- Dissemination: Use the right method of dissemination; for example, instead of a top-down alert, it may require face-to-face peer persuasion or methods that create local ownership.
- Adoption: Recognise that implementation requires much more effort or expertise than you first think.
- Embedding: Evaluate to check for compliance and use.
- Spread: Test the solution to see if it can work elsewhere and check that it delivers in practice.

Lindland and colleagues, in a report for the FrameWorks Institute (2015), suggest the need for a 'core story' of implementation. They describe a core story as a common communications platform, which is a narrative based on evidence-based research. The core story would produce a powerful narrative of implementation to restructure how people think about the science and practice of implementation. This is a social movement tool that is then linked to a strategy. The story and the strategy combined shifts professional and public conversation about implementation. Rarely do you hear about meetings to design the implementation strategy or to talk through the factors that will help and hinder the particular intervention in its adoption and spread. The development and design of interventions are given expertise and resources but implementation, which is the make-or-break element of the intervention, is forgotten. Implementation requires both skilled expertise and concerted effort and investment. It requires improved understanding of the reasons for the lack of uptake of research findings and guidance. It needs talking about.

# Suggested Reading

*Diffusion of Innovations in Health Service Organisations: A Systematic Literature Review* by Trisha Greenhalgh, Glenn Robert, Paul Bate, Fraser Macfarlane and Olivia Kyriakidou, published in 2005. This book is of major significance for anyone responsible for implementation. As Sir Liam Donaldson says in his foreword, it genuinely breaks new ground in conceptualising and mapping a vast intellectual terrain in a way that provides insight and adds practical value. This book is a towering work of remarkable scholarship. I could not have put it better myself.

## Chapter 11

# The Next Fifteen Years and Beyond

Are you really listening or are you just waiting your turn to talk?

**Robert Montgomery**

## Not Alone

Two things triggered this book. First was the nagging feeling that we should be rethinking our approach to patient safety, and second was something I heard in a webinar I was listening to on 27 May, 2015. Kaveh Shojania (2015) said that incident reporting *'is the single biggest waste of time in the last fifteen years'* and *'the most mistranslated intervention from aviation'*. This started my thinking, not only whether this statement was correct, but also whether there were any other aspects of patient safety that this line could be attributed to. What else had been a waste of time over the last 15 years?

When I was listening to the webinar with Kaveh Shojania (2015), he also mentioned that he was co-chairing, with Don Berwick, a review on behalf of the National Patient Safety

Foundation (NPSF) (2015) in the United States. I looked this
up. Tejal Gandhi, the CEO of the NPSF, said that they had created this review group because they wanted to galvanise the
field to move forward over the next 15 years with a unified
view of the future of patient safety to create a world where
patients and those who care for them are free from avoidable
harm. Thankfully, therefore, I was not alone in wanting to
look back at the last 15 years in order to identify what could
be done to rethink patient safety.

So what have we learnt from the last 15 years? In March
2000, the *British Medical Journal* produced a whole issue
devoted to 'Reducing Error, Improving Safety'. I still have my
much-thumbed-through copy today. This was the moment
that I genuinely thought we would truly transform the safety
of patient care. A journal devoted to patient safety was
extremely rare at the time. The editor, Richard Smith, stated
in his editorial that it is essential that doctors, patients and
politicians worldwide grasp the scale of the problem, and in
their article, 'Safe Healthcare: Are We Up to It?', Lucian Leape
and Don Berwick (2000) wrote about the 'error prevention
movement'. In a prophetic statement, they said that '*making
more fundamental and lasting changes that will have a major
impact on patient safety is much more difficult that simply
installing new technologies*'. They told us that there were no
'quick fixes' and that it was important to redesign our many
and complex systems to make them less vulnerable to human
error.

Leape and Berwick told us that we already knew how to
make systems safe and that, based on current available knowledge, effective changes to improve patient safety '*can begin at
once*' (Leape and Berwick 2000). These two visionaries asked
a series of important questions:

■ Will we respond adequately and fast enough?
■ Will hospitals and healthcare organisations get serious
enough, soon enough, about patient safety?

- Will they make the changes that are needed and will they be willing to hold themselves accountable for achieving improvements?
- Can we accept that patients need to know when serious accidents occur and can we honour that expectation by admitting our mistakes, investigating them and making the changes necessary to prevent them in the future?
- Are we ready to change or will we procrastinate and dissemble, to lament later when the inevitable regulatory backlash occurs?

Significantly, Leape and Berwick (2000) talked about the ability of people to talk to each other. That, as we enter the new century, a key lesson from the old should be that everyone benefits from transparency – being open and sharing information freely. That it was important to focus on culture as much as technical aspects of safety and to focus on the working conditions of staff and on how humans interact with one another. Leape and Berwick wrote this as a powerful 'call to action' to mobilise people to make safety a priority. This call to action asked us to promise patients and the public that they would not be harmed by the care that is supposed to help them; *'we own them nothing less and that debt is now due'* (Leape and Berwick 2000). For the 16 years that followed, these two leaders have repeated this mantra; they have said it in multiple different ways, but at the heart of all their work is the desire to stop patients from being unnecessarily harmed.

If you read the call to action by Leape and Berwick back in 2000, you can feel the urgency in their words; you can feel the frustration but you can also feel the hope. What did we do with that hope? Since that year, terms like patient safety, root cause analysis, systems approach to safety, safety culture and just culture have become commonplace. Across the globe, people have designed, developed and disseminated all sorts of interventions, initiatives and guidance. The language of patient safety has become embedded in that of policymakers, academics, healthcare workers and the media. Individual countries have set up national bodies and national databases to collect incidents, and there has been international guidance such as the WHO surgical checklist referred to earlier and other global campaigns such as improving hand hygiene and cleanliness. Every year, the collection of research and books on patient safety and all its component parts grows larger and larger. Patient safety has expanded to include other areas of study that can impact on the safety of patient care, including human factors, ergonomics, behavioural insights, improvement science, LEAN methodology, resilience engineering and high-reliability organisations.

Those who work in patient safety have significantly raised the awareness and understanding of patient safety and, as we have seen, some aspects of harm have been reduced. However, in the main, avoidable harm has not reduced enough and we have yet to create a systematic and holistic approach to safety. We have yet to build a safety culture that is embedded into everyday practice, everyday actions and every individual's mindset. As a result, patients are still being harmed by the same things that were happening in the year this journal was published. The reason why have I chosen to reference this particular journal, published in the year 2000, and less so the thousands of articles that have been published since is that every single article could have been written today, describing the exact same situations we still find ourselves in and have the exact same meaning for the reader.

While it feels like so much has happened since the articles were written, at the same time it feels like nothing has happened. To read these articles 16 years on is extremely sobering. What difference have we made in the intervening years? I have pulled together some comparison articles from the journal dedicated to patient safety in 2000 and how we are saying the exact same things 15 years later. These are set out in Table 11.1 as a very visible demonstration of the implementation gap, the gap between what we know should be

**Table 11.1   Comparison between the Year 2000 and the Year 2015**

| Topic | 2000 | 2015 |
|---|---|---|
| Creating a safe healthcare system | Leape and Berwick 2000 | Berwick 2015 |
| Understanding the scale and nature of harm | Weingart et al. 2000 | Hogan et al. 2015 |
| Learning from aviation | Helmreich 2000 | Macrae 2015 |
| The second victim | Wu 2000 | Berwick 2015 |
| Error reporting systems | Cohen 2000 | Shojania 2015 |
| Implementation | Nightingale et al. 2000 | Shojania and Catchpole 2015 |
| Learning from near misses | Barach and Small 2000 | Macrae 2015 |
| Human error | Reason 2000 | Reason 2015 |
| Systems changes | Nolan 2000 | Darzi 2015 |
| Investigations | Vincent et al. 2000 | PASC 2015 |

happening and what is still not. The references referred to are found in the reference section at the back of the book.

Prior to the review by the NPSF, Don Berwick was asked to lead a similar review into patient safety in England. The result was the report 'A Promise to Learn – A Commitment to Act: Improving the Safety of Patients in England', published by the National Advisory Group on the Safety of Patients in England (Berwick 2013). Berwick and the advisory group found that there was a fear in the National Health Service (NHS) that people who worked in the NHS were being blamed for the problems with systems and procedures, despite the conditions, environment and constraints they faced. The review highlighted the diffused responsibility across the NHS, and that no one clearly owned patient safety – there were too many in charge, and when this is the case, no one is. Berwick reiterated views he has stated many times before; that of making sure pride and joy in work, not fear, infused healthcare and to trust the goodwill and good intentions of the staff.

The Berwick report (2013) followed that of a public inquiry led by Robert Francis QC (2013), who had reviewed the failings in the NHS as a result of poor care in Mid Staffordshire (UK). The inquiry found a total system failure and produced 290 recommendations for change. Interestingly, the first recommendation related to implementation, that all those responsible for providing healthcare should consider the findings and recommendations of the Francis inquiry report and decide how to apply them to their own work. Each of these different parts of the NHS should state how they intend to implement them and how they intend to review them on a regular basis to ensure that any changes were embedded and sustained.

The Berwick report (2013) stated that the single most important change in the NHS in response to this report would be for it to become, more than ever before, a system devoted to continual learning and improvement of patient care, top to bottom and end to end. Additional recommendations for the future were as follows:

- All leaders concerned with NHS healthcare – political, regulatory, governance, executive, clinical and advocacy – should place quality of care in general, and patient safety in particular, at the top of their priorities for investment, inquiry, improvement, regular reporting, encouragement and support.
- The government, Health Education England and NHS England should ensure that sufficient people are available to meet the NHS's needs now and in the future. Healthcare organisations should ensure that staff are present in appropriate numbers to provide safe care at all times and are well-supported.
- The need for improved training and education (related to safety), embracing wholeheartedly an ethic of learning and creating a learning organisation. NHS leaders should

create and support the capability for learning and therefore change, at scale, within the NHS.

■ Mastery of quality and patient safety sciences and practices should be part of the initial preparation and lifelong education of all healthcare professionals, including managers and executives.

■ Development of a network of safety improvement collaborative teams to identify and spread safety improvement approaches across the NHS.

■ Patients and their carers should be present, powerful and involved at all levels of healthcare organisations, from wards to the boards of trusts, and all organisations should seek out the patient and carer voice as an essential asset in monitoring the safety and quality of care.

■ Transparency should be complete, timely and unequivocal. All data on quality and safety, whether assembled by the government, organisations or professional societies, should be shared in a timely fashion with all parties who want it, including, in accessible form, with the public.

■ Supervisory and regulatory systems should be simple and clear. They should avoid diffusion of responsibility. They should be respectful of the goodwill and sound intention of the vast majority of staff. All incentives should point in the same direction. There should be a responsive regulation of organisations, with a hierarchy of responses. Recourse to criminal sanctions should be extremely rare, and should function primarily as a deterrent to wilful or reckless neglect or mistreatment.

Two years later, the NPSF (2015) published their report 'Free from Harm: Accelerating Patient Safety Improvement Fifteen Years after *To Err Is Human*', which added to the collection of recommendations for the future. The NPSF expert panel argued that, if we are to advance patient safety, we need to shift from a reactive approach and move away from piecemeal tactics to a total systems approach to safety. The report made eight recommendations:

1. Ensure that leaders establish and sustain a safety culture.
2. Create centralised and coordinated oversight of patient safety.
3. Create a common set of safety metrics that reflect meaningful outcomes.
4. Increase funding for research into patient safety and implementation science.
5. Address safety across the entire care continuum.
6. Support the healthcare workforce.
7. Partner with patients and families for the safest care.
8. Ensure that technology is safe and optimised to improve patient safety.

## How Did We Get Here?

I asked myself, what would I do differently for the next 15 years? What keeps me awake at night, what frustrates me, what would I like to change? I landed on three areas:

- Are we learning?
- What is the right culture for safety?
- Can we narrow the implementation gap?

In answer to the question, are we learning? We have explored together the growth of patient safety and seen how early pioneers were not listened to, despite, some might think, compelling evidence. We have discovered the problem with incident reporting and incident investigation. We have found that we are really good at counting– creating league tables, pie graphs and trend data of incident reports. But we are not learning. We know from countless stories and worldwide experts that the best people can make the worst mistakes, healthcare systems will never be perfect and human beings will never be perfect. We should expect to administer ten times the dose of a drug, expect to operate on the wrong leg; if we anticipate all of these and more and have a preoccupation with failure and learning from failure rather than counting where we have failed, then we will start to change things.

I shared my own experience of administering ten times the dose of a drug and how this error is repeated time and time again. The single key lesson from my own personal story was the failure to learn from it. I have said earlier that there was a presumption on my part – and that of my colleagues – that the error was as a result of incompetence. There was no investigation because the solution was for us to be less incompetent. Even that was badly handled; if it was incompetence, should I not have received extra training or increased supervision? Everything simply carried on as if nothing had happened. None of us talked about what happened. In order to learn, we needed to talk to each other about what had happened. One of the solutions would have been to have had conversations that encouraged people to talk together about what could be done differently. If we had had these conversations, people would have learnt more about what they could do to make their care safer and, as I said earlier, if we had done all of that, who knows how many children could have been saved from harm?

In answer to the question, what is the right culture for safety?, this book has explored the just culture for safety and reminded us all of the now infamous statement by Lucian Leape (1997), that the '*single greatest impediment to error prevention is that we punish people for making mistakes*'. We learnt about the tragic story of Kimberley Hyatt, which shared so many parallels with mine. We heard how she blamed herself, how she told others she would be more careful in the future, but how she was stopped from practising her beloved nursing and how this ultimately led to her taking her own life.

Can we narrow the implementation gap between the ideal and the real? There are key messages and learning points for the next 15 years:

- Patient safety and a safety culture are a way of being.
- New ideas take time to embed and for effort to be sustained.
- Implementation is a complex process and not a one-off task or event.
- We should be tackling patient safety differently and we need to be bold enough to stop the things that are not working and start again.

Following the Berwick review (2013), the Secretary of State for Health in the UK announced three initiatives: an overarching campaign Sign Up to Safety; a network of patient safety collaborative teams; and an initiative to increase capacity and capability across the system, which is now called the Q initiative. The aim was to create a new patient safety movement to share, learn and improve ideas for creating a safety and learning culture to reduce avoidable harm and save lives. The following chapter describes our journey in one of these, the Sign Up to Safety campaign.

# Chapter 12

## Sign Up to Safety

I want today to mark the start of a new movement within the NHS in which each and every part of our remarkable healthcare system signs up to safety, heart and soul, board to ward.

**Secretary of State for Health**
*2014*

*in 'Sign Up to Safety: The Path to Saving 6000 Lives', a speech on 26 March 2014, in Virginia Mason Hospital, Seattle*

## Creating a New Movement

The ambition for Sign Up to Safety is that every hospital in England will rise to the challenge and join the campaign and commit to reducing avoidable harm. Sign Up to Safety was launched in June 2014 as a 3-year campaign to help the National Health Service (NHS) reduce avoidable harm and improve patient safety throughout the NHS, across England. With the experience of 20 years in patient safety, two years of campaigning and the benefit of time to think about what could be done differently in the future, a small group of individuals came together to design Sign Up to Safety – to create something that built on the past but also delivered something unique for the future. In particular, the design of Sign Up to Safety used lessons from a previous campaign in the UK called Patient Safety First together with social movement principles to create a locally owned, self-directed approach to improving patient safety.

Sign Up to Safety learnt a great deal from Patient Safety First, which was a campaign that ran from 2008 to 2010. While there were a number of successful aspects to Patient Safety First, it failed to create any lasting change. Despite the desire to design a bottom-up campaign, it actually became a top-down initiative. On joining, participants were told to address safety related to five areas: deterioration, critical care, perioperative care, high-risk medications and leadership. This unfortunately perpetuated the approach that continues today: tackling one harm at a time. Not only were they told what they should work on, organisations were also asked to report progress by uploading to a central database. Most organisations refused to do this.

Patient Safety First was also asked to take responsibility for the roll out of the World Health Organization (WHO) surgical checklist across the NHS in England, adding to the perception of a top-down initiative. The end of the campaign in 2010 coincided with the announcement that two of the organisations who were responsible for the campaign, the NHS Institute for Innovation and Improvement (NHSIII) and the National Patient Safety Agency (NPSA), would cease working in 2012. The lessons from the campaign remained dormant until the design of Sign Up to Safety.

The key lesson that Sign Up to Safety took from Patient Safety First (and a number of international campaigns on safety) is that bottom-up change is more likely to be successful if locally owned rather than having instruction from the top. It was important that the campaign did not tell people what to work on. In the NHS, in particular, there is a wealth of targets and central commands. What we have found is that organisations are likely to conform or comply with these in the short term but fail to embed changes for the long term. We knew from our learning in Patient Safety First that the top-down approach to safety led to providers feeling intense pressure to comply with a set of priorities, even when they did not believe that they were the same set of priorities that were important to them. The required interventions moved organisations away from their own priorities and also inhibited the increase of local knowledge and ownership of safety. So our initial challenge was to design a campaign that was genuinely not a top-down initiative.

Social movements are not created – they emerge. They often arise as a response to intolerable conditions or societal behaviours. The leaders of social movements create the conditions for others to achieve a shared purpose (Ganz 2010, Bibby et al. 2009). Social movements are dynamic, participatory and organised. One of the challenges is to provide the permission and purpose in order to get others to do the work. They are as much about interpersonal relationships that link individuals, networks and organisations than they are about formal structures. Strong movements facilitate trust, motivation and commitment. Social movements are, in the end, about changing the world, not yearning for it or just thinking about it (Ganz 2010). The greatest test is in translating the purpose into action and outcomes. Making things happen is a theme throughout this book. Surprisingly, after a while, social movements require specific measurable outcomes with real deadlines (Ganz 2010). Without this, the initial spark will simply die down and become a distant memory. These outcome measures need careful thought, as one of the main reasons movements avoid committing to specific outcomes is the fear of demotivating the people who think the movement has turned into a 'must-do' task.

Social movements think of time as an arrow. This focuses on change, beginning at a specific moment and ending at a specific moment. In the middle is the change. This 'time as an arrow' framework is more generally described as a campaign. As Ganz (2010) says, this is the most effective way to organise the most valuable resource of time. Campaigns are strategic and motivational ways to target effort and organise change activity. They unfold over time with a rhythm that slowly builds foundation, gathers gradual momentum with a few peaks along the way. The solidarity of collaborating with others in a common cause energises us. It ends when the campaign is won or lost. When it ends, we either return to normal or we regroup and perhaps undertake another campaign.

We began with a launch and a foundation period; as we gained membership we generated new resources and as motivation grew we celebrated people's stories. The campaign has instilled a philosophy of local ownership – locally owned, self-directed safety improvement by trusting members of the campaign to work on priorities that mattered to them. We told them that they were the people who knew their business or their situation better than anyone. They knew where the problems were. Organisations may not have an in-depth knowledge of safety tools and techniques but they know where their biggest risks are. Sign Up to Safety would help them by sharing the existing evidence-based interventions that would help to put things right. We would guide along the way. The campaign encouraged listening exercises with their staff, and members were invited (given the permission) to focus on a few things well and to create long-term plans. The campaign was seen as a positive opportunity to build on existing local work.

Lessons from social movement theory have been particularly important for looking at patient safety differently; crucially, the challenge of moving from motivation and mobilisation to one of action and organisation. Social movement theory has supported Sign Up to Safety to create a compelling case for change with a focus on spreading energy from front-line staff out. The campaign used the Ganz (2009) model of leadership, *the difference between leadership as a position, and leadership as a practice*, and accepted responsibility for enabling others to achieve purpose under conditions of uncertainty. One way of looking at our leadership style is to see how we reach out to mobilise the community and help them turn the campaign goals into their goals. It is a form of collaborative leadership; it is not becoming structureless (as that would be chaos) and it's about creating an interdependence between the central campaign team and the members. Ganz (2010) says that we act from habit, we don't choose, we just follow the routine and that when the routine breaks down and no one tells us what to do, we start to make real choices about our lives, communities and futures. We have found that, by not telling people what to do, we have in fact energised them. We have surprised them and some have told us they found this really exhilarating.

The Sign Up to Safety has focused on building trust with the members of the campaign. Trust that, when we said the campaign was not a top-down initiative, we were being genuine. When we invited organisations to join, we invited them to provide their own goals associated with five high-level headings that could be used as both organisational and personal pledges. We told them that their approach to the campaign would belong to them. That they were to own their work by choosing what to work on and how they would carry out that work. We told them that we would be there to cheer from the sidelines, to help them when it got difficult and to provide expertise and resources. Sign Up to Safety has therefore provided a sense of security about being organised. Being organised reminds people what needs to be done, what's important and what will happen next. It provides a rhythm for others to follow. This requires consistent coaching. Coaching avoids both micromanagement and hands-off management (Ganz 2010). At a campaign level, that means telling members what is needed before an action and during an action, and then afterwards telling them what happened. For example, we provide moments in time for members to celebrate progress with their staff. We provide them with ideas of what this could look like beforehand, help them with the actual celebration and then show pictures and stories of what people did.

To further build trust and engagement, the campaign created a brand that was synonymous with kindness, caring and compassion. In today's stressful and challenging healthcare environment, the last thing people needed was another stick. We have shown that kindness works – thanking people, valuing them and being thoughtful of all around us are vital to creating the right culture for safety and are leadership traits that we both embody and promote. The question we get asked most often is 'how can we turn the NHS and all who work in it into an organisation that cares about them?'

Key to achieving this was being positive, personalised and telling stories. The stories are about why patient safety matters, why we need to act. This is challenging when there is a great deal of inertia, apathy, change fatigue and exhaustion. We needed to find a way of giving back some hope and motivation. Stories are told. They are not messages, sound bites or brands. As we listen, we evaluate the story; we hear it in different ways depending on who the storyteller is. The storyteller will also tell it in different ways depending on who is listening. Storytelling is therefore an interaction, a shared experience, a counsel, a comfort, a challenge. For a collection of people to become an 'us' requires a storyteller, a listener and an observer (Ganz 2010). This creates a shared experience, which rarely happens in the workplace.

With a small amount of finite resources and a tiny team, we compensated for resources with resourcefulness. Hope is what allows us to deal with problems and is one of the most precious gifts we can give each other and the people we work with (Ganz 2009). Being hopeful is about being positive, clear and consistent. Messages supported by powerful personal narratives of individual learning inspire people to keep going. Stories can make a significant contribution to personal and professional growth as they communicate our values through the language of the heart: our emotions (Ganz 2009). Everyone, whether providing healthcare, monitoring, inspecting, guiding or commissioning, should do so with a positive purpose, providing hope and energy that inspires rather than crushes. One source of hope is the experience of credible solutions – not just the theory, but direct experience of what could work (Ganz 2010). We have therefore started to experiment with a method of experiential learning using conversations and storytelling. Sharing stories are a great way to learn. Another source of hope is relationships. We have therefore tested conversations and storytelling by gathering people together and sharing their challenges, obstacles and how they learned to overcome them. Stories that demonstrate how they are implementing their plans, stories to illustrate the impact of local activity for safety, stories about how they overcame a challenge: stories of possibility.

Social movements also counter feelings of isolation with a feeling of belonging. Sign Up to Safety has created a brand for people, not only to trust, but to belong to something. By promoting our membership numbers, individual organisations could see that they belonged to something that was both growing and considered meaningful by others. In the first 2 years, membership has grown to over 400 NHS organisations. Over the first 2 years, the members have been provided with numerous online and downloadable resources. Our model has a central hub of organisers that are connected to all of the member organisations through a safety lead. We have created a virtual community, bringing people together via stories, newsletters, blogs and webinars; building awareness and knowledge across the safety community and guided towards a shared vision and goal.

A good campaign can be thought of as a symphony of multiple movements that adapts to the rhythm of change (Ganz 2010). Sign Up to Safety has evolved and grown as time has progressed. So during the course of the campaign, we have been constantly reviewing patient safety research, guidance and thought pieces, and seeking knowledge that would help us develop and share with our members to help them too. We have visited and spoken to large numbers of our members and started to have a conversation with them about what it feels like to do safety improvement in the NHS, what it feels like to be them – the challenges, the barriers and what works. The campaign team itself has learnt a lot about leadership and teamwork. For example, to address the challenge of decision-making, which at times veered from autocracy to consensus, we introduced ways of working that enabled each other to engage thoughtfully around our shared cause.

The main focus for the campaign has been to address the following three areas:

- How are we learning?
- What is the right culture for safety?
- Can we narrow the implementation gap?

## What Have We Learnt So Far?

Over the last 2 years, the Sign Up to Safety team has found that

- Staff are blamed even when they haven't been given the chance or conditions for success.
- Focusing on quality rather than safety has shifted the emphasis away from the fundamentals of safety science.
- Bad news is unwelcome, and too often silenced.
- We fail to listen to staff and patients.

We have embraced the recommendations of the Berwick report (2013) and the many recommendations by others over the last 2 years. In December 2015, Don Berwick, in a keynote speech he gave in Orlando, called for a new era in patient safety, one which he says should be called the moral era (Berwick 2015). That we have experienced the era of science and discovery in the 1990s and early 2000s. That we have moved into the second era of accountability, measurement, control and punishment and the erosion of trust. We agree that the moral era should include the actions recommended by Berwick:

■ Stop excessive measurement; that is, not to stop measuring, but to 'tame' measurement. Berwick suggests reducing current metrics by 50%, and then when that has been achieved, consider reducing them again by another 50%.
■ Abandon complex incentives; that is, suspend complex incentive programmes for individual healthcare workers, especially for doctors, nurses and therapists. He says if a programme is too complicated to understand, too complicated to act upon by getting better, then it isn't an incentive programme. It's a confusion programme.
■ Decrease focus on finance; that is, focus on the needs of patients and their families.
■ Avoid professional prerogative at the expense of the whole; that is, move away from 'It's my operating room time'; 'I give the orders'; 'Only a doctor can'; 'Only a nurse can'; as these habits and beliefs die very hard and they're not needed.
■ Recommit to improvement science; that is, study improvement such as process control charts and PDSA (plan-do-study-act) methodology.
■ Embrace transparency; that is, share anything we know about our work with the people and communities we serve – 'what we know, they know, period'.
■ Protect civility; that is, stop making jokes about herding cats, green eyeshades, soulless bureaucrats, bed blockers, the surgical personality or the demanding patient.

■ Listen. Really listen; that is, coproduction, patient-centred care and finding out what matters to patients (and staff) should be the new balance of power – the authentic transfer of control over people's lives to the people themselves.

It is this last recommendation of Don Berwick (2015), *Listen. Really Listen*, that has stimulated our thinking in the Sign Up to Safety team and reawakened us to a potential answer to our frustrations. We have learnt a lot from astonishing people along the way – clinicians and patients or family members of patients who had been harmed. Over time, we started to get a sense that people just didn't have the time to do the things they wanted to and that, in particular, they didn't feel they could share their concerns, their feelings or their ideas. They told us that they felt they were not listened to, that their ideas and concerns were being squashed or silenced or ignored.

The world is becoming more technological complex; we have the ability to talk to people across the world, not only instantly, but also face to face. Smartphones and social media keep people connected in ways we could only imagine two decades ago. There is also a growing generational and cultural gap in the way people communicate with each other and the different channels they use. We assume we know how to conduct a conversation – after all, we have been doing it all our lives.

I believe that we can change the safety culture in healthcare if we start listening to one another again. Listening to another human being starts to create a relationship, starts to help us understand them more. The reason why I believe this so fervently is that 'not listening', 'not being heard' or 'not being able to speak out' has led to harm on numerous occasions. Listening means we hear someone else's point of view rather than forcing our own onto others. We move away from our judgments and assumptions towards curiosity. This means we start to learn more about what could be safer, what could or should be changed.

However, because healthcare in the main has become so complicated, solutions like having a conversation is seen as far too simplistic; so instead of taking it at face value, we try to turn it into a tool or a new technique and in turn make it more complex and difficult than it needs to be. People assume that you need specialist knowledge and a toolkit or guideline that will tell you what to do. In this world of complex interventions, people become suspicious if it looks too straightforward. The simple solution is rejected as a result.

A safety culture is reliant on people being able to speak up and talk to each other about what they notice and what they think others should know. It is reliant on trust, openness, honesty, forgiveness, kindness and compassion. The most important aspect of creating the right culture is to learn to listen. To listen to patients and the people who care for them. It could be the difference between getting it right and getting it wrong.

# *Chapter 13*

# Enlightenment

The single biggest problem in communication is the illusion that it has taken place.

**George Bernard Shaw**


## Profound Simplicity

William Schultz argued in 1979 that understanding progresses through three stages: superficial simplicity, confused complexity and then profound simplicity. Profound simplicity is achieved when people doubt the completeness of their assumptions, and through experimenting with a wider variety of possibilities may realise that out of that confusion may come a fuller understanding of what they face (Weick 2009).

My own knowledge has moved from superficial simplicity as a risk manager in the 1990s. The superficial simplicity in risk and patient safety included the notion that we should imitate aviation and other high-risk industries with incident reporting, culture change and attention to communication and teamwork. In the beginning, those who worked in patient safety thought that improving safety would be achieved by capturing errors and incidents, easily learning from them and then simply sharing that learning for all to change their practice. We thought that by simply disseminating good practice, everyone would read it, learn from it and change their practice. We thought that checklists would be simple interventions that everyone in healthcare could use.

Confusing complexity arrived quickly after this with multiple safety interventions, multiple alerts, safety targets, must-do solutions, unclear and conflicting evidence of what works and a constant cry for sustained implementation. With regard to checklists, we did not realise how complex it actually was to implement them, how much it needed a change to the way people work together and the way they view each other – implementation required an understanding of resistance to change, behavioural change theories and issues like hierarchy.

It is natural to struggle with periods of confused complexity, and the field of patient safety is no different to others. Weick (2009) suggests that, when we are confused, we pay closer attention to what is happening in order to try to reduce the confusion. This contemplation helps us see that our initial simplifications were superficial, and we also see that some of those initial simplifications still hold true, although for different reasons than we first thought. These new simplifications help us make sense of the earlier confusion and are what we now term as profound simplicities or wisdom. Profound simplicity arises from a deeper knowledge and understanding of what is happening.

Profound simplicity is only achieved by working through the confused complexity, and this needs to be lived – experiential learning is vital. Without that, people have no idea why the simplifications are profound, why they work or what lessons there are. Without this lived experience, the borrowing is superficial and typically fails when implemented (Weick 2009).

Only now do I think that we are moving into the era of profound simplicity, where we are starting to realise that there are some fundamental and seemingly simple aspects related to how we work in patient safety that could make a profound difference to the safety of patient care. This brings me to the Sign up to Safety campaign's work to transform the safety culture in healthcare through helping people talk to each other. Hopefully, you will feel I have left the best till last.

# Our Throughline

While preparing for a particular talk I was due to give, I read Chris Anderson's (2016) recent and outstanding book, *TED Talks: The Official TED Guide to Public Speaking*. He devoted a chapter on what was titled the throughline. He talked about how every talk needs to say something meaningful, but somehow they leave the audience with nothing to hold on to. They may have beautiful slides and charismatic stage presence but no real takeaway. He suggests applying a tool that is used in plays, movies and novels, which is to use a throughline. This, he says, is the connecting theme that ties together each narrative element, and that every talk should have one.

I really liked this idea as a way of bringing to life the third year of the campaign, Sign up to Safety. So we spent a day working through what we wanted out throughline to be. We wanted to construct something so great that it would create a strong thread throughout all the elements of our work. A way of connecting everything together. Chris Anderson suggested a good exercise which we all used: to try to encapsulate our throughline in no more than 15 words. Those 15 words needed to inspire our members but also focus them on the precise idea we wanted to work on. We came up with:

*We want people to talk to each other about what they know about keeping patients safer.*

## Our Solution for Change Is Conversations

At the very heart of what we do in healthcare and at the very heart of patient safety is being able to talk to each other.

Talking to each other underpins and is vital for a safety culture. Talking to each other means a conversation. Something we feel is done really badly when times are pressured and people are stressed. When conversations go wrong it can lead to so many poor outcomes. At the very worst, it can mean a patient may die as a result. A good conversation should allow people the time to speak, listening with intent and asking clarifying questions and observing what is being said and what is not. Talking to each other requires a set of values and behaviours: being kind, caring, thoughtful, honest, respectful, authentic, being human, telling the truth, creating trust, being fair and showing love and appreciation. Talking to each other can also be disruptive, confrontational, challenging and move people from one view to another, moving from the same thing every day to something new.

We wanted to help people feel proud, help people understand reality and possibility and hope that things can be better to help people understand what it feels like day to day and help them tackle the limitations and ultimately the permission to act, share information, shine a light on good practice, help celebrate what is being done and inspire.

We wanted to connect with people in a kind and human way that acknowledges the conditions and possibilities for safer care and to work with and through people in an authentic manner. Our throughline would help us honestly explore both people's lived reality and new possibilities, enquiring more deeply into how to make people safer. It builds on our work originating from the 'beneath the surface' experiments and provides a framework for the next stage of that work, gaining more insight into the possibilities that conversations can have to help people with their daily dilemmas.

This work builds on all our work to date. It helps continue to build the just culture for safety, empower people to take local ownership of safety and make the most of scarce resources. There is also a sense of urgency, that if we get this right we may be able to help people with the pressure and stress they are currently feeling. The following story is from a junior doctor who wished to remain anonymous (Guardian 2016). It is told in their own words:

> I'm scared, I'm exhausted, and I hate being a doctor. This was not the plan. Sat on the kitchen floor of our flat, tears poured down my face as my partner looked on, stunned and worried. My third day on the wards was over, and I never wanted to go back.
>
> I'd certified the death of my first patient – examining the cold body of a woman I had cared for, trying to forget that this was also my first time in a mortuary. I'd struggled to draw blood from patients who didn't deserve my trembling, wide-eyed persona stuttering towards them with a needle. I'd welled up with tears as I sat in front of a computer trying desperately to remember how to prescribe a drug, paralysed with the knowledge of the harm that could befall my patients if I got it wrong.
>
> Throughout medical school, I had been told that my foundation years – the first two years of a doctor's career – would be totally different to my training. I expected to be thrown in at the deep end, but I expected to be supported. I expected a well-oiled team around me, keeping an eye on me, never leaving me feeling alone. Sat at that computer – the only doctor on the ward on my second day in the job, praying no one would ask me anything – I was clueless, exhausted, and had no idea what to do about it.
>
> On our first day on the wards as new doctors, the more senior doctors were also new to the hospital. This was also the case on the second day. The well-oiled team was not there – it hadn't even been created yet. After years of scribbling in notes, and learning to prescribe on neatly laid-out forms, I was faced with a computer system I'd never used, on

which I was expected to request every test and order every drug.

I barely spoke to any patients as I followed my consultant on the ward round. I then sat at the computer, and wished, as I ham-fistedly hit the keyboard, that I had learned to type properly as a child. I tried not to think about how the patient who had reduced fluid intake was still taking in more water than me that day.

After finishing my jobs, which was only achieved two (unpaid) hours after I was supposed to end for the day, I did a quick walk round the ward, to make sure I hadn't missed anything with my patients, to reassure myself that it was ok to leave them to the similarly overstretched night team. Patients and relatives seemed glad to see me, asking questions about their care, commenting on my having been there for 12 hours already (though none of them seemed surprised).

That walk-around was probably the only reason I made it back in the following day. Having the chance to speak to the people I was trying so hard to care for, I was able to glimpse the reasons why I'd started my training – that I would help people, that I would learn from my patients, that I would make a difference. That night, my partner arrived home to find me passed out on our bed, still wearing my coat, my microwavable supper still in the fridge.

I received my rota for this job three days before it started. Only then was I able to confirm whether I could attend my oldest friend's wedding at the end of August. A week in, I still have no contract, and no one can tell me how much I can expect to be paid. My parents and partner are keeping me in food and rent until the end of August and my first payday, and I have no idea when I'll be able to start paying them back.

I hope and pray it will get better. We already know that gaps in rotas caused by understaffing are bigger than ever. The whole NHS seems to be teetering on a precipice, with everyone ploughing on, but unable to ignore that this is unsustainable without proper funding and better staffing.

Many of my patients don't need to be in hospital. They need to be in the community, where they are less likely to be stuck in bed for hours, less likely to contract the infections that, despite our best efforts, will always populate hospitals full of sick people. But social care is in even worse shape than the NHS, so we're having to pick up the slack (and the cost). 'It's always a baptism of fire,' people tell me. 'That's how you learn.' But I don't want to risk people's health for the sake of my own education. I'm scared. I'm already exhausted. I'm not sure I want to be a doctor anymore, and I've only just begun.

The one key lesson from this story and all of the stories I have shared throughout this book is that we need to find a way for people to talk to each other. This doctor needed desperately to talk to someone about how they were feeling and for someone to listen intently to them so that they could carry on.

People are too busy, too stressed, running from one task to the next. The doctor talked about the one thing that kept them going which was to have the chance to speak to the people they were caring for and, in doing so, this conversation reminded them of why they wanted to be a doctor in the first place. A conversation, one human being to another, reminded them of who they are.

As shown in Figure 13.1, we need to move from the personal responsibility approach to safety, 'it's all down to me', to one of public-wide responsibility and acceptance, 'this affects all of us and therefore we all need to act'. We are exploring

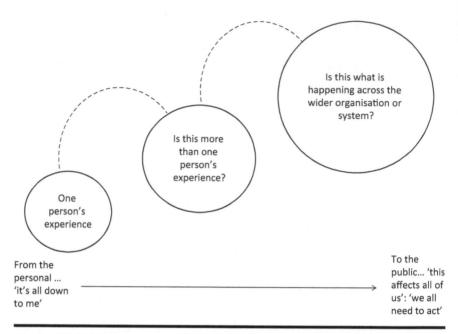

One
person's
experience

Is this more
than one
person's
experience?

Is this what is
happening across the
wider organisation or
system?

From the
personal ...
'it's all down
to me'

To the
public... 'this
affects all of
us': 'we all
need to act'

**Figure 13.1  Using one person's experience to learn about the system.**

and experimenting with methods to move the conversation
from one person's experience to the conversations of teams
or units, and to use this learning to impact on organisational behaviours and even system-wide strategies for making
care safer.

Our assumptions at the moment are that by simply talking
to each other we will achieve the wider cultural change that
everyone has been striving for. This is profoundly simple. Do
less telling, learn to listen, learn to ask the right questions and
acknowledge what is being said and heard. Margaret Wheatley
talks about how people band together with their colleagues
and friends to create the solutions for real social change. Such
change, she argues, will not come from governments or organisations, but from the ageless process of thinking together in
conversation (Wheatley 2009).

# Chapter 14

# An Evolving Concept

Slow down and take your eyes off the computer.
Look at the patient in the bed and listen.

**Sorrell King**

## Good Conversations

A good conversation is where the person is given the time to speak, someone listens and, importantly, hears so that they can respond. Asking the right questions and listening empowers the other person in the conversation and draws them in. If we combine conversations that really matter with the desire of the front line to improve the future, we have a powerful force for change from the ground up. We have the potential for something great. If we help people talk to each other, one good conversation that matters could shift the direction of change forever.

Everyone and anyone, staff, patients, families, those who work in or receive healthcare – we all need to talk to each other. What we mean by that is to hold meaningful conversations, allowing people the time to speak, really listening to someone with intent and asking clarifying questions where needed and noticing what is being said and what isn't. People know their own situations better than others, they know the challenges and opportunities they face – they just need help to have that conversation.

In safety, we want people to talk to each other about the implementation gap or when they think something is unsafe or when something has gone wrong. But we are not doing this, we are not talking to each other about what we know about keeping people safer; we are not listening and we are not noticing what should and could be done differently. We have seen how Ernest Codman tried to encourage people to listen to each other using group conversations about patient outcomes through the use of morbidity and mortality meetings. His ideas were dismissed by his colleagues. We have seen how Josie's parents were not listened to and how Sorrel King, Josie's mum, now offers advice to other healthcare staff: *'slow down and take your eyes off the computer. Look at the patient in the bed and listen. Listen to that mother who is saying something is wrong'*. We have seen the impact on the Morrish family when things went so badly wrong and when asking even straightforward questions about why their child died was met with hostility and resistance. Fundamentally, the inability to ask the right questions and to listen means people are not learning for the future.

There are many examples that show how badly things can go wrong if we don't talk to each other more effectively and what happens when we are not listened to, we fail to listen or we fail to learn. In the stories threaded throughout this book, there are key moments that could have changed those stories forever. If Bob Ebeling had been listened to, he may have been able to prevent the deaths of seven astronauts. If the anaesthetist caring for Richie William had articulated his concerns more clearly, he may have been provided with better information from the haematologist on what he needed to do and it may have made him aware of the dangers of injecting vincristine into the spine. If Josie's mum had been listened to,

Josie's dehydration and deterioration may have been identified in time. Listen to the mums, the daughters, the husbands and the patients themselves. If they are worried or question an action, listen. Don't be too proud and too late.

As Sam Morrish's story tells us, we make it really hard for the patients and the families to find out simple answers. The patient or the person who accompanies them knows their own story – they may not know the answers but they know how they feel. Make patients and colleagues feel their voice is worth listening to. Sam's story also tells us how really hard it is for clinicians to have a conversation between themselves and patients, one human to another. People who work in healthcare fundamentally want to do a great job, and if we get the right culture where staff can feel supported when things go wrong and are able to speak out when they are concerned about safety, we will be able to learn about what we can do differently to make care safer.

## A Variety of Methodologies: The World Café Story

In order to understand how conversations could help shape a safety culture, the Sign Up to Safety team reviewed a number of methodologies, one of which is the World Café. In *The World Café: Shaping Our Futures through Conversations* (Brown and Isaacs 2005), there was one story that particularly resonated. This was the story of Bob Veazie, a senior engineer at Hewlett-Packard. Bob's role was to improve organisational performance. He experienced a World Café event where he realised that the boxes in his traditional hierarchical organisation chart would be better depicted as webs of conversations. That managing these conversations might not be the best way to achieve results. He described how, every day, his teams were engaged in conversations about different questions. He sensed the power and potential of networks of conversations and how the connections among them could produce real value. He wondered if conversations and personal relationships were at the heart of our work. He questioned his role as the leader, and whether he was contributing to or taking energy away from this natural process. He questioned why we are using the intelligence of just a few people when we could gain the intelligence of hundreds or thousands of people.

When Bob became the safety leader for Hewlett-Packard's inject operations, he was eventually responsible for 50,000 employees at five sites around the world. When he started, there was a high accident rate. This varied from country to country; in Oregon, United States, 6.2% of the workforce was being harmed each year, and 4.1% in Puerto Rico and 2.5% in Ireland. The initial attempt to address this was to implement a programme called STOP, which is where people give each other feedback about how they are doing against a list of predetermined risks. Feedback from the test group was that the discussions related to someone else's list, not their own ideas about what their own risks really were. He says, we started with someone else's answer rather than a question that should have evoked people's own curiosity and creativity. The second attempt was to pull together a small group of full-time internal safety experts, called safety change agents. The safety change agents defined the set of risks for the whole organisation. As Bob says, this was the second mistake. He felt that, by doing the work internally, they were consistent with the principles of the World Café; that the wisdom lies with the people themselves. In reality, they had created a small group that functioned like outside experts, removing the responsibility from others.

The third attempt was to ask, what are the few key questions that would improve safety results if we were to ask them to people already in conversations about their daily work? What they chose to do was pose key safety questions to the people in the already existing but invisible 'café' – the web of relationships – so that they could integrate the questions into conversations they were already having. Bob and his team began by meeting with people where they normally gathered, in staff meetings, worker assemblies and on the shop floor. First, they shared the local facilities' safety record with them. They showed these people the visual from the World Café that shows how one person can then influence a small group, who can then influence a number of groups, which can lead to large-scale impact. This shows the powerful pattern of the World Café in action. It helped employees realise that, to make a shift, rather than use predetermined training programmes that focused only on solutions, that what they actually needed to do was focus on the problems together and bring multiple different view points towards the aim of thinking, feeling and acting differently. It demonstrated that they were trusted to hold conversations and develop relationships and mutual intelligence as a way of dealing with critical safety questions.

The first question Bob and his team explored was: *'if you were to get hurt, how would that happen?'* People began answering the question with risks that they identified from their own work situations. The second question was: *'do you want to manage these risks before people get hurt or after?'* Of course, they all said, 'before'. The final question was: *'what do you want to do about it?'* Bob's team had invited them into a meaningful conversation called *'I don't want to get hurt at work'*. They talked together about different methodologies, their own ideas for managing risk. Then they were asked to try out the answers, keep asking the questions and revisit the answers as they learnt more.

Bob used the World Café as a guide to help his safety effort and articulated this as an ongoing 'Safety Café', a network of conversations across the company connected by key questions. The internal safety experts he had employed were used as the hosts. Bob and his team travelled across the world, sharing the stories and bringing together people from across the product lines to learn with and from each other. Bob says that, as they were leading the safety effort, they were simultaneously learning about how conversations are a core method that really works to enhance performance. The results of these efforts were that the accident rate reduced in Oregon from 6.2.% to 1.2% while Puerto Rico went from 4.1% to 0.2%. The company as a whole was able to reduce the overall accident rate by approximately 33%.

There is a particularly interesting aspect to this story. Bob was moved from his safety role to another in the organisation. Since then, the safety rate has begun inching back up, particularly in Oregon, which has gone from 1.2% to 2.5% – still better than the original 6.2% but not as good as Puerto Rico, which has remained at 0.2%. Bob believes that there is a difference between the two sites in particular. In Puerto Rico, they continued to host the same number of conversations on safety issues, whereas Oregon reduced the numbers of conversations. He concluded (Brown and Isaacs):

> In a world that is always dynamic and changing, what kind and level of conversational leadership is needed to create long term sustainable performance on any key issue of systemic importance, whether it be safety, quality or a new development.

Synergies between Sign Up to Safety and the Hewlett-Packard story:

- We went out and about to where people normally worked – local hospital events and staff meetings.
- We started by asking them to review their own safety record.
- We have trusted the member organisations to work on what matters to them and to hold conversations about critical safety questions.
- We have trusted them to create their own relationships and networks.
- We have talked to them about what a good conversation looks like.

- Change starts with an individual but needs to shift from that individual to small groups, then larger groups, then the whole organisation and system beyond.
- We have chosen to focus on questions rather than the answers or solutions.
- We have shared stories across multiple sites and professions.
- We have brought people from across the healthcare system rather than working with components of it.
- We believe that conversations are a core method that really works to enhance patient safety and a safety culture.
- In a National Health Service (NHS) that is dynamic and constantly changing, we need to ensure that we create a long-term approach for sustained change – we need to keep up the relentless focus.

## Methods Used to Date for Patient Safety Conversations

An incident report represents someone speaking up, sharing their concerns. Rather than simply completing a form and waiting for information to be fed back, we could consider a different approach, a way in which there is open conversation, participative investigation and a collective approach to learning – gathering people together to talk about what went wrong. There are a number of ways in which this can be done: an after-incident review, an after-incident briefing and a multidisciplinary huddle.

For many, we need to be invited to speak and share our ideas and opinions. There are a number of tried and tested tools and techniques in healthcare that have created the space for people to come together in order to speak and share. These include

- Huddles
- Briefing and debriefing

Huddles take a variety of formats and are used for a variety of purposes. Huddles are about people coming together to talk for about 10 minutes on issues that can affect the whole organisation. This can include representation from operational services – catering, cleaning, portering, procurement and so on. A huddle connects people and can help drive the organisation-wide culture change needed to improve safety and quality across the board. A huddle can be reactive; for example, it can be triggered by an event such as a patient fall. A huddle gathers people together to quickly assess how the fall could have been prevented, what can be learnt from it and what could be done differently in that moment – a real-time conversation rather than a full debrief. Huddles can be proactive, preventing patient safety issues and staff concerns (O'Brien et al. 2016). In this case, a huddle gathers the team together to talk about the day, the shift or the next few hours. This is different from the beginning of the day briefing because it can happen at any point of the day. Different types of huddles include

■ Formalised huddles: Planned huddles at specific times with attendance being mandatory in a designated area and with the huddle facilitated by the most senior person.
■ Information-capturing huddles: Using tools such as a 'huddle sheet', which can list the areas of discussion such as a list of patients with indwelling catheters, a list of patients at risk of falling and so on.
■ Unplanned impromptu huddles: Called at any time to regroup or seek collective advice and can be called by anyone from the team. This could even happen in a patient's room – for example, if they have fallen, it is a way of assessing the environment in real time with everyone inputting their views on what could have been done differently.

Briefings are short gatherings, usually at the beginning of a day, a shift, a clinic or session; basically, any duration of event or time that involves working as a team. It can take as little as 30 seconds to conduct a briefing and should be no longer than 15 minutes. A briefing is best complimented by a debriefing at the end. They both work well if people understand that individuals will behave differently but that these different roles or behaviours should be valued and respected and are all equally important. There needs to be a process of linking and therefore learning from one to the other. Issues highlighted in the morning briefing, for example, can be then discussed at the huddle and then through to the debriefing, checking in and taking the pulse of the department at any given time. They need to be helpful, focused and create a shared understanding of what is needed and when.

## Factors That Hinder a Good Conversation

Everyone should be given the chance to express their opinions freely and safely but there are a number of factors that get in the way of an effective conversation, including

- Personalisation
- Lack of respect
- Hierarchy
- Grandstanding
- Gender
- Bullying

People are naturally prepared to look for causes of events to find explanations. They do this through personal storytelling. Stories provide examples of our experiences. We attribute causes to these stories and, as long as the cause and effect make sense, we accept them and use them to try to understand the future. Sometimes, these assumptions are wrong and the actions taken fail to prevent something from happening again in the future (Norman 2013). Instead of trying to come up with a solution too quickly, we need to slow people down and explore in more detail what people are saying in their stories.

Don Norman (2013), in his excellent book, *The Design of Everyday Things*, describes in depth the problems of human error and the use of design to help humans succeed. It also tells us a lot about how we need to help people talk more about their daily lives. This is recommended reading for anyone interested in this aspect of patient safety. He provides numerous stories, and one of them illustrates design and human error very simply. He tells us that he was once asked by a computer company to evaluate a new product. He spent the day learning to use it and trying it out on various problems. With this particular keyboard to enter data, it was necessary to differentiate between the 'return key' and the 'enter key'. If the wrong key was pressed, the last few minutes' work was irrevocably lost. He pointed this out to the designer, explaining that he had made the error frequently and that it was likely that others were making the same mistake.

The designer's initial reaction was to question Don on why he made the error and why he didn't read the manual. The designer then proceeded to provide Don with a detailed explanation of the different functions of the two keys. Don explained that he did indeed understand the two keys but that he had simply confused them. He told the designer that they had similar functions and were located in similar locations; that a skilled typist would probably, as he had done, hit the 'return' automatically without thought. The designer said that no one else had raised this as an issue and that the employees had been using the system for months. Don and the designer then went to talk to a few of them. He asked them if they had ever hit the 'return key' instead of the 'enter key', which resulted in them losing their work as a result. They said yes, that it happened a lot.

Why didn't anyone say anything about it? They had been encouraged to report any problems with the system. Don considered that it was because it was a human error. That they were happy to report when the system wasn't working or there was a problem with the technical aspects of the computer but when they pressed the wrong key they assumed it was all down to them. The employees felt they had simply been erroneous and would do better next time. As Don says, the idea that a person is at fault when something goes wrong is deeply entrenched in today's society. Don Norman again reminds us, as James Reason, Lucian Leape and Don Berwick has, that humans continually make mistakes – it is an intrinsic part of being human. People are not machines – they are constantly interrupted, they have to bounce between tasks and return to tasks at a later time, possibly skipping a step or two. Our strengths are our ability to adapt and be creative rather than being precise and mechanical.

Don Norman suggests that we eliminate the term human error and instead talk about communication, interaction and collaboration between human and machine or human and task. The designers of both tasks and machines have a special obligation to understand how people behave and how they will interact. Designers should strive to minimise the chance of inappropriate actions but also maximise the chance that this can be discovered and rectified. When people interact with machines, things will go wrong and it should be expected, anticipated. This requires talking to each other and constantly understanding what could be done differently to make things safer.

Simply asking the questions is only one aspect; it is also important to ask them in a respectful, caring and kind way. As Schein tells us (2013), what we ask and the way in which we ask, together with the way in which we respond, is ultimately the basis of building trusting relationships. Schein tells us that trust, in the context of a conversation, is believing that one person will acknowledge the other, that they will not take advantage of each other, not embarrass or humiliate and that they will tell the truth. This again reminds us of the issues of psychological safety or creating a safe space. Through having a good conversation, individuals can start to build trust, learn together and get even better at communication with each other and their patients. Respect is also found in acknowledgement. Acknowledgement is in our words and in our actions, including body language. Not looking someone in the eye, bowing our heads when someone else speaks, not smiling when a smile is needed, showing no recognition of the other person's feelings – all of these are a lack of respect and acknowledgement.

Hierarchy is a significant issue in healthcare. There are rules and boundaries that exist in relation to a good conversation; we are not supposed to interrupt the boss; we are not supposed to question the expert surgeon or the senior nurse. But for the safety of patients, this can be extremely damaging. While a concerted effort has been made in healthcare to remove this risky behaviour, we still hear of cases where someone failed to point out a particular risk that sadly led to a patient being harmed as a result.

There is nothing more potent than being in the presence of someone who just wants to listen to you. That is, someone who is both open minded and open hearted, someone who does not get restless for you to find a solution or for you to take up their preferred solution. There is therefore something really irritating about someone who is not listening to you and simply waiting their turn to speak. Too often, I attend meetings or conferences where individuals come and talk to me and tell me exactly what the problem is and what should be done to put it right. This telling approach is described by Edgar Schein (2013) in his book *Humble Inquiry: The Gentle Art of Asking Instead of Telling*. Some people find it very difficult to give up on their certainties, their positions, beliefs or self-explanations. Schein says that we need to remove our bias towards telling as we tell too often, and even when we are asking questions, we are often just telling. Each of us needs to try to unfreeze our fixed positions or move away from the entrenched views and assumptions we have long held; there is no room for high horses or grandstanding. Moving away from an attachment to a particular point of view opens us up to hear different perspectives and shift from polarised positions or ideas. This is particularly hard for people to do – they tend to need help to shift from one of advice-giving to asking open questions. Too often, people speak as if they knew already the complex situation another person is describing and that their preferred solution, developed elsewhere, could be 'down-loaded' and would work.

Gender is another important aspect to focus on. We talk a lot about the ability or inability to speak out crucial to a safety culture. However, we rarely talk about this in terms of gender. We think we have increasing equality but it still falls short of the ideal. This can have a profound effect on safety. Across the many cultures worldwide, women find it really hard to speak out, often only giving an opinion if asked. Gender and the impact on patient safety should be openly acknowledged rather than lurking beneath the surface. There is so much fear that speaking up will make the situation worse or be inappropriate or go unheard. All of us, men and women, have a role to play. Women need encouragement and respect from both men and other women. We need to act as a cohesive group, working together for a common purpose.

Our words are powerful – they can hurt and they can encourage. A bullying culture is extremely inhibitory; why speak up when you could get blamed or punished for doing so? Bullies can stifle conversations and shut down others in a number of ways. Telling individuals what to do puts the other person down; it implies that the other person is ignorant and assumes that the other person does not know. A living example of '*are you really listening or just waiting your turn to talk*' is the meetings that are held across the NHS in England to discuss whether certain incidents are avoidable or unavoidable. They are usually around pressure ulcers or falls. The meetings are supposed to be about learning why they happened and what could be done to prevent them. On the face of it, that sounds ok, doesn't it? However, let's look at this in a bit more detail. The meetings all relate to whether the pressure ulcer was avoidable or unavoidable. Individuals (mainly nurses) stop what they are doing and nervously trickle into a room, clutching mounds of paper with sweaty hands, to argue their case for whether the incident they were involved in was avoidable or unavoidable. A group of nurses sit as judge and jury and debate each case. The individual nurses are desperate to be put in the unavoidable camp. This, at best, is distracting and, at worst, perpetuates the blame and fear culture. People feel that they can't deliver the bad news or problems without retribution. This approach is also too simplistic and stifles people who need to share the problems in order to identify the potential learning and solutions.

## Suggested Reading

*The Power of One, the Power of Many* (bringing social movement thinking to health and healthcare improvement) by Jo Bibby, Helen Bevan, Elizabeth Carter, Professor Paul Bate and Glenn Robert, published in 2009.

*The World Café: Shaping Our Futures through Conversations*, written by Brown and Isaacs in 2005.

# Chapter 15

---

# Facilitated Conversations

---

There is nothing more potent than being in the presence of someone who just wants to listen to you. Someone who is both open minded and open hearted; someone who does not get restless for you to find a solution or for you to take up their preferred solution.

**David Naylor**
*2015*

## Facilitated Conversations to Narrow the Implementation Gap

We recognise that people and relationships are at the heart of patient safety and that a structured and facilitated conversation could draw them together to help them listen and hold a profoundly different conversation about what we can all do differently. The facilitation of experiential learning and reflection is challenging, but a skilled facilitator, asking the right questions and guiding reflective conversation before, during and after an experience can help open a gateway to powerful new thinking. While it is the learner's experience that is most important to the learning process, it is also important not to forget the wealth of experience a good facilitator also brings to the situation. A key aspect of our learning is as much about the process, the method and the skills needed to facilitate as it is about the learning of the actual conversations themselves.

The Sign up to Safety experiments are rooted in an explicit approach to learning, co-consultancy, coaching and World Café methodologies (Naylor et al. 2016). We have used a method that has enabled people to have the time to talk together, to create a sense of curiosity but also to free them up from the pressure to reach a conclusion. These are simply conversations; not advising, coaching, mediation, negotiation or problem-solving – just simple conversations. It is not about fixing, it is about listening and through that listening, learning about what could be done differently next time.

The approach helps people pause and look at the situation in more depth and more carefully than they have done before, and to notice what has happened. This has led to ideas and insight that could improve patient safety. A vital component of this work is to help people share a story and listen to one another to develop ideas and insights.

In order to create an accurate picture of what is going on, we need to recognise that we each see something different because of who we are and where we sit. Only when we have many different perspectives do we start to know what is going on. This requires values such as respect and appreciating that individuals from diverse backgrounds, differing levels of seniority, different genders and professions come with a rich and diverse knowledge, and that all voices are equal.

## Trio Methodology

In October 2015, the Sign Up to Safety team tested a method to try and understand what is really going on when we try to make things safer for patients. This we described as the trio methodology. The event was to explore with front line National Health

Service (NHS) staff what we could do to narrow the 'implementation gap', or why there is often a difference between what should happen and what actually happens. We titled the event 'getting beneath the surface', that is, getting beneath the surface of our superficial ideas about why there is this gap and identifying the more fundamental and perhaps core reasons why it exists. Current methods of huddles or briefings and debriefings are relatively short and more about information sharing than they are about really exploring a problem in depth.

The trio methodology is where individuals work in threes. Working in groups of three, provided the structure for a conversation between two people and for one person to observe what is going on. At the beginning of the event, the team demonstrated the trios so people could see a live example. Each of the three individuals has a different role; one person starts by sharing their story, one is an active listener who will ask clarifying questions of the storyteller and the third is an observer who will carefully observe what is being said and what is not being said.

Figure 15.1 provides a visual demonstration of how the trios met three times throughout the course of the day. This enabled people to rotate across the different roles and for everyone to have their chance of sharing a story.

The speaker told a story from their own experience. The active listener asked clarifying and open questions to help the speaker to develop their story, to help them go further. It

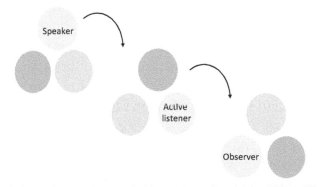

**Figure 15.1    Trio methodology.**

was not about giving advice or saying what should have been done – it was simply to encourage the speaker to say more. Some prompts were used:

- What did you notice?
- Does that happen normally?
- How can you use that to do something differently?
- What were others doing and saying?
- What do you think was really going on?
- What did you feel?

The observer listened in silence, as if behind a one-way mirror. As they listened, they were asked to pay attention to their thoughts and feelings and consider

- What explanations about what is going on are offered and implied?
- What is missing, silent or absent from this account?

To summarise what was being heard, we used a novel aspect – the use of metaphors to help build and connect from one story to another (Naylor et al. 2016). At the end of the session, each observer was asked to offer a metaphor that somehow captured some aspect of the story. The use of metaphor was initially met with confusion and cynicism but this quickly moved to one of appreciation when, after the first round, the metaphors were discussed and the participants could see how beautifully a metaphor can capture exactly what the story is trying to say. Metaphors such as 'hitting my head against a brick wall', 'pushing a boulder uphill' or 'feeling stuck in the fog' resonated with the participants in relation to their struggles to make care safer.

Metaphors are more integral to our language than we first realise. It is often through metaphors that we communicate with each other but we are often not aware of using them because we take them for granted and have begun to treat them as literal. Metaphors have the effect of both describing and constructing our realities. By describing a situation through a metaphor, we not only give it a rich identity but also help clarify for others exactly what we are talking about. The use of metaphors seems to transcend or at least help with the language barrier and the potential for things being 'lost in translation' between the individual participants. We are very good in healthcare at using confusing or 'in-house' language that can confuse and silence others around us.

For this first event, the trio conversations were interspersed with a number of different groups: a 'large group' of all participants, which was facilitated and met three times during the day, and a number of 'small' groups of individual participants who met in between the three conversations. The first large group was to welcome everyone, help people make the transition from work demands into a more reflective place, introduce the roles and ensure people understood the role they were agreeing to take up throughout the day and why. The second large group was to check that everyone was feeling ok and they were happy to continue with the second and third trio. The final large group was to hear and record the most important insights/observations from each small group.

There were three small group meetings. The purpose of these was to help us gather what people were noticing over the course of the day. The three small groups were made up of the people who took up the same role in the trio rounds: Small Group 1 was made up of all the people who go first as Speakers; Small Group 2, the Active Listeners and Small Group 3, the Observers. As the day progressed and as each person experienced the different roles, our learning about the method grew and grew. The method seemed to create what some describe as 'psychological safety' and lessened inappropriate grandstanding.

There were three rounds of conversations as trios as follows:

Round 1: 35 minutes
    Person A is the Speaker and they talk for 20 minutes
        around their 'safety story'

Person B is the Active Listener

Person C is the Observer, who at the end of the
20 minutes offers their metaphor to describe what they
have heard and records it on a flip chart

Round 2: 35 minutes

Person C becomes the Speaker and tells a story

Person A becomes the Active Listener

Person B is the Observer, who at the end of the 20 minutes offers their metaphor to describe what they have
heard and records it on a flip chart

Round 3: 45 minutes

Person B becomes the Speaker and tells their story

Person C becomes the Active Listener

Person A becomes the Observer, who at the end of the
20 minutes offers their metaphor to describe what they
have heard

The process is simple, yet can lead to unexpected results.
Using conversations supports a core human need of being able
to share our stories and to be heard – it is amazing what can
happen when you provide a simple but profound format for
people to really talk together as equals. We learnt that, if you
ask people in a supportive setting to tell their story, they will.
People can be incredibly generous, imaginative and open-
hearted. If you get some willing, able and thoughtful people
into a good place to work, then it is possible for them to
develop a useful theory about what may work better in their
local context. They can also learn quickly. Trios are a way of
exploring safety issues without repercussions, where people
can experiment with roles and behaviours that are beyond
their daily habitual ones and also one where they can extend
their compassion to those in need (Naylor et al. 2016). What
we found was humbling – that one of the easiest human acts,
of listening to someone, simply listening, can also be the most
healing.

# Quad Methodology

Since the first event, we have carried out a number of different experiments in order to develop a set of principles that can be adapted for use by all. We are constantly designing and developing activities to help people talk to each other, notice more, speak out more and share more about what is really going on when things work well and when they go wrong. If we can do this, we believe we will make progress on narrowing the implementation gap and thus help to make people safer.

A second experiment added a fourth person, a Recorder, as shown in Figure 15.2. These we have obviously named as quads. The fourth role of the Recorder is to help the group capture and record the key pieces of information of what is being said and what is not, and any insights and ideas as well as capturing the metaphor that the Observer has described. This role was added to address the issue that we found in the trio work, which was that the conversations remained private to the group of three rather than being made open for all to learn from.

# Fishbowl Methodology

In another experiment, shown in Figure 15.3, we used the relatively tried and tested 'fishbowl' method. We used it to

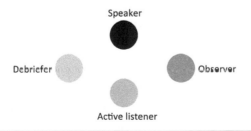

**Figure 15.2　The quad methodology.**

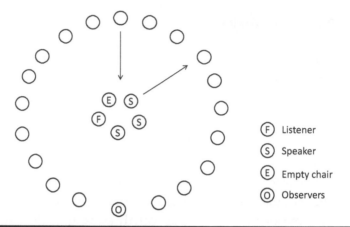

**Figure 15.3   Fishbowl methodology.**

bring clinicians and patients and family members of patients who had been harmed to talk together. Initially, we started with a large circle for all attendees. Six chairs were arranged in an inner circle and the remaining chairs were left in a circle outside the inner circle. Four clinicians were invited to fill the inner circle while the rest of the group sat on the chairs in the outer circle; one chair was left empty. This method requires a highly skilled facilitator who can help the participants engage with each other safely.

The audience in the outer circle listened in on the discussion without interrupting the conversation. However, during the conversation, any clinician could, at any time, step forward and occupy the empty chair, thereby joining the conversation in the inner circle. When one person moved, an existing member of the inner circle voluntarily left and freed a chair. The discussion then continued with clinicians entering and leaving the inner circle.

The second phase of the conversation occurred after around 30 minutes, when the inner circle turned to face the outer circle and the facilitator led a discussion between the two circles. After about 20 minutes of this, the inner circle then turned back to talk to each other about what they had heard in the discussion.

The fishbowl method we used sought to create what some describe as 'psychological safety'. The discussion focused on investigations. What we found was that people, whether they are the clinicians or the patients, ultimately want the same thing: to be listened to, to be heard and to have a conversation – one human being to another.

## Small Group Conversations

In a further evolution, we have tested the use of groups of six. This is where one person tells their story, one person is the active listener asking questions and one person is assigned the role of providing a debrief or recording the key messages. The rest of the group are Observers. The story is told in 20 minutes and then people discuss what they heard for 10 minutes and give feedback to the other groups in the room. This process could then continue for a number of rounds so that a variety of different people can share their story. The benefits of this approach are that it lends itself to the introverts and reflectors of the group who may struggle to share a story or be a speaker but may still gain a significant amount from listening and observing others sharing theirs. It recognises that, even if people are silent, there is a huge amount of learning that can take place. It also closely replicates day-to-day activity and behaviours.

## Large Group Conversations

Let's revisit the question that Bob Veazie asked: why we are using the intelligence of just a few people when we could gain the intelligence of hundreds or thousands of people. The experiment we are in the process of working on and designing is to use everything we have learnt to run an all-day event, replacing the traditional conference format to one that has been designed to be highly interactive and participative. This will move people away from running an event where the perceived experts are placed on a platform to distil their wisdom to a relatively passive audience.

We believe that conferences need to move away from relentless PowerPoint presentations and speeches from 'deemed' experts on a stage to a more participative conversational approach that helps the audience work together on complex challenges and questions. We are designing an event that is turning a conference on its head; where the participants and audience are the speakers and the speakers are there to observe. This is an attempt to genuinely use the wisdom of the audience together with the topic experts to talk together and build a collective wisdom. The assumption is that those in the room individually have pieces of the answer and when those pieces are joined up we can see the potential.

Conversational events can be used to bring people together from across the spectrum of professions and hierarchy, from either within a healthcare organisation or across different organisations, to talk about particularly challenging issues. This approach to learning helps create a culture of sharing and a common purpose, and has huge potential for developing the foundations for mutually respectful, kind, understanding teams – vital for a safety culture where staff can feel able to speak out and listen to each other.

Surprisingly, people need to develop the skills for conversations, which are best learnt through experience. People have become so used to the pressures of imparting information quickly and succinctly that they find it hard to tell their story in detail. They need encouragement to realise that they have a valuable story to tell and that there is so much more to that story than they think. Equally, a problem-solving rather than a coaching style of management and leadership encourages people to interrupt and provides them with a suggested solution or with the answer. Active listening is a hard skill to master, to think of questions that will elaborate what is being heard rather than shut the storyteller down. Active listening is about being silent for the most part and then asking the occasional clarifying question. It is not about steering the conversation or influencing what is being said from the perspective of the listener – it is about trying to encourage more information from the person who is speaking, taking the story further and further. It is also not about answering, providing advice or implying any particular solution for the speaker. Clarifying questions include how did you feel about that, what reactions did you have to that situation, what would you have liked to have done differently, why did that happen, what may have caused this, what have you tried so far, what are you going to do next? They are questions that the storyteller has to answer with an explanation or a feeling, rather than a straightforward yes or no.

Then we come to observing what is being said and what is not being said; this needs to be practised. It requires skills to notice the language used, the level of detail and what both the storyteller and the active listener are finding hard to get to the bottom of or to get beneath the surface of the story. It requires a freedom of thought and the use of our creative side and imagination to be able to visual what they are hearing in the form of a picture, an image or a metaphor.

## What We Have Learnt

Essentially, all of these methods are ways in which we can help people tell their stories, help people listen and help people ask really helpful questions without judging. These methods help with different learning styles and different personalities – helping the introvert be reflective, helping the extrovert share their feelings and so on. Over time, we have learnt a number of useful principles about helping people talk to each other. The initial three key lessons are

**One:** Pay attention to the detail and as much attention to the preparation as to the method.

The aim should be to ensure people feel valued, respected and cared for, in a mindset whereby they will feel able to talk, listen and observe what is being said and what is not being said. Important factors for this include a warm welcome and introduction; an expert facilitator; introductions that don't create superiority or hierarchy; and processes that create energy, insight and ideas. What we knew intuitively and now recognise consciously is that attention to detail is important. People need the time to arrive, to slow down, to enter a more reflective frame of mind and, importantly, to feel and to be valued.

The **organisers** need to

- Provide sufficient detail about the event for people to make an informed choice about participation
- Provide a comfortable environment and venue
- Purposefully organise the day to take care of the participants so that they can focus their energy on the task in question
- Carefully think through the selection process
- Provide consistent and clear communications all the way through from the invite through to the feedback; be genuine and friendly at registration

**Two:** Use the right method for the particular circumstances.

The variety of methods described here are simply different methods to help people talk to each other. The method chosen will depend on the size of the group, the size of the room and the question or questions you want to answer.

The **designers** need to

- Use a facilitating structure. The trio method worked in that it provided a structure that helped people talk differently and where there was occasional surprise about what new insights emerged via the metaphor and subsequent conversations.

■ Use a method that helps people move from a 'look back' to thinking in the present. In other words, a story is a construction of a complex set of events that reflects the assumptions of the teller – it's easy to accept your own version as the complete truth.

■ Use a method that enables learning. We concluded that some insights were lost to the private domain. As a consequence, these insights into what was really going on, in terms of the lived experience of leading safety innovations, could not be fully explored, elaborated or articulated.

■ Frame the dilemma as a question rather than a problem – seek to identify the right question to answer, a question that if explored thoroughly will provide the breakthrough you are seeking; a question that generates hope, new thinking and action for the future rather than keeping us focused on the past and obstacles.

**Three:** Use skilled facilitation.

Everyone's contribution should be encouraged. This isn't just about sharing a story and receiving support, this is about careful and skilled facilitation.

The **facilitators** need to

■ Ensure everyone feels safe
■ Demonstrate the method to help reduce the sense of performance or learning anxiety *('I don't want to look stupid')* that trying something new can evoke
■ Allow people to be free of finding an answer, making it explicit that we the process is not about looking for a particular outcome
■ Slow everything down
■ Reduce the hindering factors of power and hierarchy by using first names rather than full names, titles or roles

- Create a structure that is focused around listening and helping each other to listen better
- Help 'pull' from the private to the public domain
- Value those who don't obviously contribute and who are not the first to speak – these are people who listen and see patterns from simply paying attention

# Conclusion

It may seem to some that the race for patient safety has just begun, but the patience of the public we serve is already wearing thin. They are asking us to promise something reasonable, but more than we have ever promised before; that they will not be harmed by the care that is supposed to help them. We owe them nothing less, and that debt is now due.

**Leape and Berwick**
*2000*

Everything we do should be about keeping patients as safe as we can, and the vast majority of healthcare is provided safely and effectively. However, just like any high-risk industry, as we have seen in this book, things can and do go wrong. The field of patient safety has grown exponentially over the last 15 years and there is such richness in the early thinking of human error and patient safety that remains as important today as it did when it was first published. That thinking has laid the foundations for where we are today.

Patient safety or improving the safety of patient care is not simple or straightforward – there is no easy solution or one thing we should be doing. The next few steps we take in patient safety will need to unite all the different and equally important component parts so that we make much bigger strides together. The answer exists not in any one of us, but in all of us; we are not the experts and nor should we look to other experts. The answers lie all around us, in those who are working day to day in healthcare.

There is a need to respect patient safety as a unique science that needs scientists, people who have expert knowledge in one or more fields of patient safety. Safety is not a task or a set of technical interventions; it is not notices on the wall or a risk register – it is a mindset, it is in everything we do. As we have learnt here, feeling safe means we need to be constantly vigilant, noticing what happens every moment of every day, noticing when it goes right and noticing when it doesn't. With that knowledge, we can then constantly adapt our behaviour and practice.

Rather than feeling like we have failed, we need to see the moment we are in as a huge opportunity. The last two decades have succeeded in creating the wider conversation, to open people's minds to the dangers of healthcare, the risks of what we do every day and the potential for what we do to go wrong. It has opened people's eyes to the scale and nature of the problem. Improving patient safety has, at long last, risen high on people's agenda but we are now acutely aware of how our early interventions were too simplistic and that we then moved into an era of complexity that, with all the best intentions, left a lot of people behind.

This book has made the case for going back to basics to revise the very foundations of risk and patient safety, to focus on the small shifts, small changes or small steps that can be made in order to incrementally make a difference over a longer period of time. This is not the time for quick wins, short-term projects or focusing on one harm at a time. Help everyone by breaking down the enormity of the task into bite size pieces. Provide hope with stories of what other people are doing.

I have had the privilege of being able to ask some key questions, the kind of questions that in fact you can only ask when you have the hindsight of experience and past efforts. It is only through this hindsight and these experiences that I believe we can finally see what we might want to do or where we now should be focusing. The answers are helping us move into the era of profound simplicity. We need to think and act differently in many ways, but at the very heart of safety is people. And at the core of people and relationships are conversations. Our profoundly simple approach is to build a culture of safety that helps people to talk to each other about what they know about keeping patients safer.

Listening to another human being starts to create a relationship, starts to help us understand them more. Listening means we hear someone else's point of view rather than forcing our own onto others. We move away from our judgments and assumptions towards curiosity. This means that we start to learn more about what could be safer, what could or should be changed. The reason why I believe this so fervently is that, as the stories threaded throughout this book tell us, 'not listening', 'not being heard' or 'not being able to speak out' has led to harm on so many occasions.

What we need is a culture of kindness, one that is based on a very simple premise: that we all need to learn to talk to each other again. At the heart of it all, patient care and patient safety, there are human interactions, relationships and conversations. If we get this right, we will go a long way to transforming safety for future patients and those who care for them. As I have mentioned earlier, in writing about his life in error, Jim Reason says that he has discovered two key principles:

- Learn as much as possible about the details of how people work.
- Most importantly, never be judgmental.

In my 30 odd years' experience in healthcare, 20 or so working in patient safety, I have discovered three key things:

- Only by learning to truly listen to others will we find the answers.
- Relationships are the difference between safe and unsafe care.
- If you do nothing else, be kind to others. In patient safety, that means caring for those who have been harmed but also caring for those who have caused the harm. It means talking to each other with respect and being friendly, generous and considerate. Kindness is about being open-hearted towards everyone – no matter who they are – and especially those in need, not because you want something in return but because they need it.

In this life we cannot always do great things. But we can do small things with great love.

**Mother Teresa**

# References and Further Reading

Amalberti R, Auroy U, Berwick D, Barach P (2005) Five system barriers to achieving ultrasafe health care free. *Ann Intern Med* 142(9): 756–764.

Anderson C (2016) *TED Talks: The Official TED guide to Public Speaking*. London: Headline Publishing Group.

Anon (2000) Looking back. *BMJ Qual Saf* 320: 812.

Baker G, Norton P, Flintoft V, et al. (2004) The Canadian adverse events study: The incidence of adverse events among hospital patients in Canada. *CMAJ* 170: 1678–1686.

Barach P, Small S (2000) Reporting and preventing medical mishaps: Lessons from non-medical near miss reporting systems. *BMJ Qual Saf* 320: 759–763.

Berkes H (2016) Your letters helped challenger shuttle engineer shed 30 years of guilt. NPR Radio and Colby Itkowitz, *Washington Post*. February 25 2016.

Berwick DM (1989) E. A. Codman and the rhetoric of battle: A commentary. *Milbank Q* 67(2): 262–267.

Berwick DM (2013) A promise to learn: A commitment to act; Improving the safety of patients in England [online], available at https://www.gov.uk/government/publications/berwick-review-into-patient-safety.

Berwick DM (2015) The moral era conference [online speech], available at: https://www.youtube.com/watch?v=DKK-yFn7e_0).

Bibby J, Bevan H, Carter E, Bate P, Robert G (2009) The Power of One, the Power of Many: Bringing Social Movement Thinking to Health and Healthcare Improvement. Coventry: NHS Institute for Innovation and Improvement. ISBN 978-1-906535-82-7.

Bickford Smith PJ (2001) Designing safer medical devices requires financial and political support. *BMJ* 322: 548.

Brahams D (1991) Manslaughter and reckless medical treatment. *Lancet* 338: 1198–1199.

Brennan TA, Leape LL, Laird NM (1991) Incidence of adverse events and negligence in hospitalized patients: Results of the Harvard medical practice study. *N Engl J Med* 324(6): 370–384.

Briant R, Buchanan J, Lay-Yee R, et al. (2006) Representative case series from New Zealand public hospital admissions in 1998–III: Adverse events and death. *N Z Med J* 119: 1909.

Brown J, Isaacs D (2005) *The World Café: Shaping Our Futures Through Conversations That Matter.* San Francisco: Berrett-Koehler.

Catchpole K (2013) Spreading human factors expertise in healthcare: Untangling the knots in people and system. *BMJ Qual Saf* 22(10): 793–797.

Chantler C (1999) The role and education of doctors in the delivery of health care. *Lancet* 353: 1178–1181.

Cohen MR (2000) Why error reporting systems should be voluntary. *BMJ* 320: 728–729.

Darzi A (2015) The NHS safety record needs to be as good as the airline and motor industries. *Health Service Journal.* Accessed on line via hsj.co.uk on 11 February 2015.

Davis P, Lay-Yee R, Briant R, et al. (2002) Adverse events in New Zealand public hospitals I: Occurrence and impact. *N Z Med J* 115: 268–271.

Dekker S (2012) *Just Culture.* Aldershot: Ashgate.

Dekker S (2014) *Safety Differently: Human Factors for a New Era, 2nd edn.* Boca Raton, FL: CRC Press.

Dekker SWA, Leveson NG (2014) The systems approach to medicine: Controversy and misconceptions. *BMJ Qual Saf* 24: 7–9.

Department of Health (2000) *An Organisation with a Memory.* London: The Stationery Office.

Department of Health (2006) *Safety First.* London: The Stationery Office.

Dixon-Woods M, Pronovost PJ (2016) Patient safety and the problem of many hands. *BMJ Qual Saf* 25 (7): 485–488.

Donabedian A (1989) The end results of health care: Ernest Codman's contribution to quality assessment and beyond. *Milbank Q* 67: 233–256.

Donaldson LJ (2004) When will health care pass the orange-wire test? *Lancet* 364: 1567–1568.

Dyke RW (1989) Treatment of inadvertent intrathecal injection of vincristine. *N Engl J Med* 321: 1270–1271.

Eccles M, Mittman B (2006) Welcome to implementation science. *Implementation Science* 1 (1) doi:10.1186/1748-5908-1-1 [online], available at: http://implementationscience.com.

Elwyn G, Taubert M, Kowalczuk J (2007) Sticky knowledge: A model for investigating implementation in healthcare contexts: A debate. *Implementation Science* 2: 44 [online], available at: http://implementationscience.com.

Francis R (2013) Report of the Mid Staffordshire NHS foundation trust public inquiry [online], available at http://webarchive. nationalarchives.gov.uk/20150407084003/http://www.midstaff-spublicinquiry.com/sites/default/files/report/Executive%20sum-mary.pdf.

Ganz M (2009) Why stories matter [online] Speech adapted from a presentation at Sojourners' Training for Change Conference in June 2008, available at sites.middlebury.edu.

Ganz M (2010) *Leading Change in Handbook of Leadership Theory and Practice.* Edited by N Nohria, R Khurana. Boston: Harvard Business Press. ISBN 13: 9781422161586.

Gawande A (2002) *Complications.* New York: Picador.

Gawande A (2009) *The Checklist Manifesto: How to Get Things Right.* Bungay: Clays.

Girling AJ, Hofer TP, Wu J, et al. (2012) Case-mix adjusted hospital mortality is a poor proxy for preventable mortality: A modelling study. *BMJ Qual Saf* 21: 1052–1056.

Greenhalgh T, Robert G, Bate P, Kyriakidou O, Macfarlane F, Peacock R (2005) *How to Spread Good Ideas. A Systematic Review of the Literature on Diffusion, Dissemination and Sustainability of Innovations in Health Service Delivery and Organisation.* London: NHS Service Delivery Organisation.

Guardian (2016) (Anon) I'm a new junior doctor and I already hate my job. *Guardian* [online], available at: https://www.theguardian.com/healthcare-network/views-from-the-nhs-frontline/2016/aug/15/new-junior-doctor-already-hate-job?CMP=fb_gu.

Haines A, Donald A (1998) The NHS's 50th anniversary, getting research findings into practice: Making better use of research findings. *BMJ* 317: 72–75.

Hall MJ, Levant S, DeFrances CJ (2013) Trends in inpatient hospital deaths: National hospital discharge survey, 2000–2010. *NCHS Data Brief* (118): 1–8.

Haynes AB, Weiser TG, Berry WR, et al. (2009) A surgical safety checklist to reduce morbidity and mortality in a global population. *N Engl J Med* 360: 491–499.

Heinrich HW (1959) *Industrial Accident Prevention: A Scientific Approach*, 4th edn. New York: McGraw Hill.

Helmreich RL (2000) On error management: Lessons from aviation. *British Medical Journal* 320: 781.

Hignett S, Jones EL, Miller D, et al. (2015) Human factors and ergonomics and quality improvement science: Integrating approaches for safety in healthcare. *BMJ Qual Saf* doi:10.1136/bmjqs-2014-003623.

Hogan H (2015) The problem with preventable deaths. *BMJ Qual Saf* 25 (5): 320–323.

Hogan H, Healey F, Neale G, Thomson R, Vincent C, Black N (2012) Preventable deaths due to problems in care in England acute hospitals: A retrospective case record review study. *BMJ Qual Saf* 21: 737–745.

Hogan H, Zipfel R, Neuburger J, Hutchings A, Darzi A, Black N (2015) Avoidability of hospital deaths and association with hospital-wide mortality ratios: Retrospective case record review and regression analysis. *BMJ* 351: h3239.

Hollnagel E (2014) *Safety-I and Safety-II: The Past and Future of Safety Management*. Farnham: Ashgate.

Hollnagel E, Woods DD, Leveson NG (2006) *Resilience Engineering*. Abingdon: Ashgate.

Hunter DJ (2002) Decision-making processes for effective policy implementation discussion paper [online], available at http://www.nice.org.uk.

Huxley E (1975) *Florence Nightingale*. London: Chancellor Press.

Institute of Medicine (1999) *To Err is Human: Building a Safer Health System*. Washington, DC: The National Academies Press.

Jeffcott SA, Ibrahim JE, Cameron PA (2009) Resilience in healthcare and clinical handover. *BMJ Qual Saf* 18: 256–260.

Jones El, Lees N, Martin G, Dixon-Woods M (2016) How well is quality improvement described in the perioperative care literature? A systematic review. *Jt Comm J Qual Patient Saf* 42(5): 196–206.

Kliff S (2016) Fatal mistakes [online], available at http://www.vox.com.

Landrigan CP, Parry GJ, Bones CB, et al. (2010) Temporal trends in rates of patient harm resulting from medical care. *N Engl J Med* 363: 2124–2134.

Leape LL (1994) Error in medicine. *JAMA* 272: 1851–1857.

Leape LL (1997) Testimony, United States Congress, House Committee on Veterans' Affairs, Dr. Lucian L. Leape, MD, October 12, 1997.

Leape LL, Berwick DM (2000) Safe healthcare: Are we up to it? *BMJ Qual Saf* 320: 725–726.

Leape LL, Brennan TA, Laird N, et al. (1991) The nature of adverse events in hospitalized patients: Results of the Harvard Medical Practice Study II. *New Engl J Med* 324: 377–384.

Leary T (1991) *The Game of Life*. New Falcon Publications.

Leveson NG (2012) *Engineering a Safer World: Systems Thinking Applied to Safety*. Cambridge, MA: MIT Press.

Lilford R, Edwards A, Girling A, et al. (2007) Inter-rater reliability of case-note audit: A systematic review. *J Health Serv Res Policy* 12: 173–180.

Lindland E, Fond M, Haydon A, Volmert A, Kendall-Taylor N (2015) *Just Do It: Communicating Implementation Science and Practice. A FrameWorks Strategic Report*. Washington, DC: FrameWorks Institute.

Macrae C (2014a) Early warnings, weak signals and learning from healthcare disasters. *BMJ Qual Saf* 23: 440–445.

Macrae C (2014b) *Close Calls: Managing Risk and Resilience in Airline Flight Safety*. Basingstoke: Palgrave Macmillan.

Macrae C (2015) The problem with incident reporting. *BMJ Qual Saf* 25(2): 71–75.

Makary M, Daniel M (2016) Medical error: The third leading cause of death in the US. *BMJ* 353: i2139.

Marx D. (2001) *Patient Safety and the Just Culture: A Primer for Health Care Executives*. New York, NY: Trustees of Columbia University.

Marx D (2009) *Whack-a-Mole: The Price We Pay for Expecting Perfection*. Plano: By your side studios, available at http://www.whackamolethebook.com.

Mayer E, Flott K, Callahan R, Darzi A (2016) NRLS Research and development [online], available at www.imperial.ac.uk/patient-safety-translational-research-centre.

Mills DH (1977) *Report on the Medical Insurance Feasibility Study*. San Francisco: Sutter Publications.

Mitchell I, Schuster A, Smith K, Pronovost P, Wu A (2016) Original research patient safety incident reporting: A qualitative study of thoughts and perceptions of experts 15 years after 'To Err is Human'. *BMJ Qual Saf* 25: 92–99.

Morrish S (2015) Personal statement by Scott Morrish (CCF0079) [online], available at http://data.parliament.uk/writtenevidence/committeeevidence.svc/evidencedocument/public-admin-istration-committee/nhs-complaints-and-clinical-failure/written/18025.html.

National Audit Office (2005) *A Safer Place for Patients: Learning to Improve Patient* Safety. London: The Stationery Office.

National Patient Safety Agency (NPSA) (2004) Seven steps to patient safety: Summary guide [online], available at http://www.npsa.nhs.uk

National Patient Safety Agency (2005) Seven steps to patient safety: Primary care [online], available at http://www.npsa.nhs.uk.

National Patient Safety Agency (NPSA) (2008) Using vinca alkaloid minibags (adult/adolescent units). Rapid response report. National Patient Safety Agency. NPSA/2008/RRR04.

National Patient Safety Foundation (2015) Free from harm: Accelerating patient safety improvement fifteen years after to err is human. National Patient Safety Foundation, Boston, MA; 2015 [online], available at http://www.NPSF.org.

Naylor D, Woodward S, Garrett S, Boxer P (2016) What do we need to do to keep people safer? *J Soc Work Pract* [online], available at http://www.tandfonline.com/eprint/bVgSRFVSIpjh8cwp2Gka/full.

NHS Confederation (2016) Key Statistics on the NHS [online], available at http://www.nhsconfed.org/resources/key-statistics-on-the-nhs [Accessed 24 March 2016].

Nightingale PG, Adu D, Richards NT, Peters M (2000) Implementation of rules based computerised bedside prescrib-ing and administration: Intervention study. *BMJ* 320: 750–753.

Nitkin K, Broadhead L (2016) No room for error [online], available at http://www.hopkinsmedicine.org/news/articles/no-room-for-error.

Noble DJ, Donaldson LJ (2010) The quest to eliminate intrathecal vincristine errors: A 40 year journey. *BMJ Qual Saf* 19: 323–326.

Nolan TW (2000) System changes to improve patient safety. *BMJ Qual Saf* 320: 771–773.

Norman D (2013) *The Design of Everyday Things*. London: The MIT Press.

O'Brien CM, Flanagan ME, Bergman AA, et al. (2016) 'Anybody on this list that you're more worried about?' Qualitative analysis exploring the functions of questions during end of shift hand-offs. *BMJ Qual Saf* 25: 76–83.

Panesar S, deSilva D, Carson-Stevens A, et al. (2015) How safe is primary care? A systematic review. *BMJ Qual Saf* doi:10.1136/bmjqs-2015-004178.

PASC (Public Administration Select Committee) (2015) Investigating clinical incidents in the NHS: Sixth Report of Session 2014–15 Report [online], available at: http://www.publications.parliament.uk/pa/cm201415/cmselect/cmpubadm/886/886.pdf.

PHSO (Parliamentary and Health Service Ombudsman) (2016) Learning from mistakes: An investigation report by the parliamentary and health service ombudsman into how the NHS failed to properly investigate the death of a three-year child [online], available at http://www.ombudsman.org.uk/__data/assets/pdf_file/0017/37034/Learning-from-mistakes-An-investigation-report-by-PHSO.pdf.

Pronovost PJ, Berenholtz SM, Goeschel C, et al. (2008a) Improving patient safety in intensive care units in Michigan. *J Crit Care* 23: 207–221.

Pronovost PJ, Berenholtz SM, Needham DM (2008b) Translating evidence into practice: A model for large scale knowledge translation. *BMJ* 337: 1714.

Pronovost PJ, Cardo DM, Goeschel CA, et al. (2011) A research framework for reducing preventable patient harm. *Clin Infect Dis* 52: 507–513.

Pronovost PJ, Cleeman JI, Wright D, Srinivasan A (2015) Fifteen years after To Err is Human: A success story to learn from *BMJ Qual Saf* doi:10.1136/bmjqs-2015-004720.

Rabøl LI, Gaardboe O, Hellebek, A (2016) Incident reporting must result in local action. *BMJ Qual Saf* doi:10.1136/bmjqs-2016-005971

Rasmussen J (1990) Human error and the problem of causality in analysis of accidents. In *Human Factors in Hazardous Situations*. Edited by DE Broadbent, J Reason and A Baddleley, 1–12. Oxford: Clarendon Press.

Rasmussen J, Duncan K, Leplat J (1987) *New Technology and Human Error.* New York: John Wiley.

Reason J (1990) *Human Error.* Cambridge: Cambridge University Press.

Reason J (2000) Human error: Models and management. *BMJ* 320: 768–770.

Reason J (2015) *A Life in Error*. Farnham: Ashgate.

Rogers EM (1983) *Diffusion of Innovations*. New York: Free Press.

Rogers EM (1995) *Diffusion of Innovations*, 4th edn. New York: Free Press.

Roos NR, Heinrich HW, Brown J, Petersen D, Hazlett S (1980) *Industrial Accident Prevention: A Safety Management Approach*, 5th edn. New York: McGraw-Hill.

Sari AB, Sheldon TA, Cracknell A, et al. (2007b) Extent, nature and consequences of adverse events: Results of a retrospective case note review in a large NHS hospital. *BMJ Qual Saf* 16: 434–439.

Sari AB-A, Sheldon TA, Cracknell A, et al. (2007a) Sensitivity of routine system for reporting patient safety incidents in an NHS hospital: Retrospective patient case note review. *BMJ* 334: 79.

Schein E (2013) *Humble Inquiry: The Gentle Art of Asking Instead of Telling*. San Francisco: Berrett-Koehler Publishers.

Scott IA, Brand CA, Phelps GE, et al. (2011) Using hospital standardised mortality ratios to assess quality of care: Proceed with extreme caution. *Med J Aust* 194: 645–648.

Semmelweis I (1857) *The Etiology Concept and Prophylaxis of Childbed Fever*. Translated by K Codell Carter (1983), Madison, WI: University of Wisconsin Press.

Shahian DM, Wolf RE, Iezzoni LI, et al. (2010) Variability in the measurement of hospital-wide mortality rates. *N Engl J Med* 363: 2530–2539.

Sheppard I, Davis J, Blackstock, D (2006) Improving patient safety by design: A new spinal/intrathecal injection safety system. *Can J Anaesth* 53: 108–109.

Shojania KG (2008) The frustrating case of incident-reporting systems. *BMJ Qual Saf* 17: 400–402.

Shojania KG (2012) Deaths due to medical error: Jumbo jets or just small propeller planes? *BMJ Qual Saf* 21: 709–712.

Shojania KG (2015) Patient safety after 15 years: Disappointments, successes, and what's on the horizon [online webinar], available at: http://www.ken.caphc.org.

Shojania KG, Catchpole K (2015) 'The problem with…': A new series on problematic improvements and problematic problems in healthcare quality and patient safety. *BMJ Qual Saf* 24: 246–249.

Shojania KG, Dixon-Woods M (2016) Response to: Medical error: The third leading cause of death in the US [online], available at http://www.bmj.com/content/353/bmj.i2139/rr-54.

Soop M, Fryksmark U, Koster M, et al. (2009) The incidence of adverse events in Swedish hospitals: A retrospective medical record review study. *Int J Qual Health Care* 21: 285–291.

Vincent, C (1995) *Clinical Risk Management: Enhancing Patient Safety.* London: BMJ Books.

Vincent C (2004) Analysis of clinical incidents: A window on the system not a search for root causes. *BMJ Qual Saf* 13: 242–243.

Vincent C (2006) *Patient Safety.* London: Churchill Livingstone.

Vincent C (2010) *Patient Safety.* Oxford: Wiley Blackwell.

Vincent C, Amalberti R (2016) *Safer Healthcare: Strategies for the Real World.* Cham: Springer Open.

Vincent C, Neale G, Woloshynowych M (2001) Adverse events in British hospital: Preliminary retrospective record review. *BMJ* 322: 517–519.

Vincent C, Taylor-Adams S, Chapman EJ, Hewett D, Prior S, Strange P, Tizzard A (2000) How to investigate and analyse clinical incidents: Clinical risk unit and association of litigation and risk management protocol. *BMJ* 320: 777–781.

Waterson P, Catchpole K (2015) Human factors in healthcare: Welcome progress, but still scratching the surface. *BMJ Qual Saf* doi:10.1136/bmjqs-2015-005074.

Weick KE (2009) *Making Sense of the Organisation: The Impermanent Organisation.* Chichester: Wiley.

Weingart SN, Wilson RM, Gibberd RW, Harrison B (2000) Epidemiology of medical error. *BMJ Qual Saf* 320: 774–777.

Wheatley M (2009) *Turning to One Another; Simple Conversations to Restore Hope for the Future.* San Francisco: Berrett-Koehler Publishers.

Woodward S (2008) From information to action: Improving implementation of patient safety guidance in the NHS. DProf thesis, Middlesex University [online], available at http://eprints.mdx.ac.uk/6920/.

World Health Organisation: Alert No. 115. 2007. Vincristine (and other vinca alkaloids) should only be given Intravenously via a minibag [online], available at http://www.who.int/patientsafety/highlights/PS_alert_115_vincristine.pdf.

Wu A (2000) Medical error: The second victim. *BMJ Qual Saf* 320: 726–727.

Zegers M, de Bruijne MC, Wagner C, et al. (2009) Adverse events and potentially preventable deaths in Dutch hospitals: Results of a retrospective patient record review study. *BMJ Qual Saf* 18: 297–302.

# Index